A Short Life of
MARTIN LUTHER

Thomas Kaufmann

Translated by Peter D. S. Krey and James D. Bratt

WILLIAM B. EERDMANS PUBLISHING COMPANY
GRAND RAPIDS, MICHIGAN

Wm. B. Eerdmans Publishing Co.
2140 Oak Industrial Drive N.E., Grand Rapids, Michigan 49505
www.eerdmans.com

Originally published in German as *Martin Luther*, 3. Auflage
by Verlag C.H.Beck oHG, München. © 2014
English translation © 2016 William B. Eerdmans Publishing Company
All rights reserved
Published 2016
Printed in the United States of America

22 21 20 19 18 17 16   1 2 3 4 5 6 7

ISBN 978-0-8028-7153-4

Library of Congress Cataloging-in-Publication Data

Names: Kaufmann, Thomas, author.
Title: A short life of Martin Luther / Thomas Kaufmann ;
    translated by Peter D.S. Krey and James D. Bratt.
Other titles: Martin Luther. English
Description: Grand Rapids : Eerdmans Publishing Company, 2016. |
    Series: Reformation resources, 1517-2017 |
    Includes bibliographical references.
Identifiers: LCCN 2016015243 | ISBN 9780802871534 (pbk. : alk. paper)
Subjects: LCSH: Luther, Martin, 1483-1546.
Classification: LCC BR325 .K37713 2016 | DDC 284.1092 [B] —dc23
    LC record available at https://lccn.loc.gov/2016015243

CONTENTS

Thomas Kaufmann's biography of Martin Luther joins a long list of life stories dealing with the friar of Wittenberg, who became Martin Luther.

This extensive interest in and preoccupation with Luther throughout the centuries is in no way surprising or unexpected. As a person both of action and profound thought, Luther attracted continuous curiosity in his life time and after his death. Since his last day in 1546, there has been no period of time when Luther suffered neglect or was overlooked and in this regard he has few peers in history. The figure of Luther has consistently aroused great hatred or an equally irresistible devotion.

The challenges for anyone seeking to compose a life of Luther or present his thought have always been considerable. Lacunae exist in his life narrative. Luther himself described some of the key events in his own biography years after their occurrence. He was not a systematic thinker, but more likely a person moved by specific events or individuals. His contemporaries were usually not indifferent to him; they were committed enemies or passionate allies.

The first biographies of Luther are practically concurrent with him and reflect this ambivalence. They disclose two trajectories that have persisted throughout the centuries. Both of these trajectories were influenced by the periods

of history through which they passed, viz. Lutheran Orthodoxy, Pietism, the Enlightenment, Liberalism, and most
recently Marxism. These trajectories could be described
as "Lutheran" or "Protestant," although not all Protestants
viewed Luther positively, and "Catholic." The latter trajectory was remarkably uniform until the last century.

Cyriakus Spangenberg, a student of Luther's, initiated
a stream of biographies that at times bordered on hagi-
ography. He was followed by such figures as Veil Ludwig
von Sechendorf in the seventeenth century, and Gottfried
Wilhem Leibniz and Gotthold Ephraim Lessing in the eigh-
teenth. In the nineteen century Georg Wilhem Friedrich He-
gel claimed Luther as a resource. In the twentieth century
Karl Holl and his students are to be credited with a Luther
Renaissance, and Karl Barth sought to understand Luther
and employ his thought. The same century saw the rise of
the Finnish School under Tuomo Mannermaa and his disciples, who argue that Luther's doctrine of justification has
affinities to the Orthodox doctrine of divinization. It was
also the time of certain Marxist interpreters of Luther, who
reflected the political situation in Europe at that time. In
addition, the twentieth century saw the appearance of note-
worthy biographies by Roland Bainton and Heiko A. Ober-
man among others. All sought from their own perspective to
present a clear account of Luther's life and thought.

The "Catholic" trajectory owes its origin to another contemporary of Luther, Johannes Cochlaeus. He saw Luther
as an infamous heretic who caused the eternal damnation
of thousands. This opinion persisted and was extended in
the nineteenth and early twentieth century by such writers
as Johannes Janssen, Heinrich Suso Denifle, and Hartmann
Grisar, whose multi volume work portrayed Luther as a dis-
turbed personality. This negative portrayal of Luther in Catholic circles began to change only with the ground-breaking

scholarship of Josef Lortz in the twentieth century, who was followed by such notable Catholic theologians as Otto Hermann Pesch, Harry Mc Sorley, Peter Manns, and Jared Wicks. These authors viewed Luther as a serious theologian and not a demented person. For them, Luther was a theologian who raised crucial questions about the nature of the Christian faith. While complete agreement with Luther is not possible from the Catholic perspective of these scholars, Luther was now acknowledged by many Roman Catholics as a consequential dialogue partner regarding Christian theology and its contemporary meaning.

This selective and concise review of history provides a sufficient background to appreciate the accomplishment of Thomas Kaufmann in his short, erudite, and intense biography of Luther. He has accepted the invitation of history to offer an account of Luther for the twenty-first century, the second century of the ecumenical movement. Its appearance in English as the 500th anniversary of the Reformation occurs provides an invaluable resource whose influence will be long lasting.[1]

WILLIAM G. RUSCH
The Divinity School
Yale University

---

1. For a fuller account of the attention given to Luther from the sixteenth century to the present, see Donald K. McKim, ed., *The Cambridge Companion to Martin Luther* (Cambridge: Cambridge University Press, 2003) 209-303, and Robert Kolb, Irene Dingel, and L'Ubomír, eds., *The Oxford Handbook of Martin Luther's Theology* (Oxford: Oxford University Press, 2014) 491-610.

1483	November 10 – born in Eisleben, Saxony; November 11 – baptism.
1484–1496/1497	Childhood and youth. First time at school in Mansfeld.
1497	School in Magdeburg.
1498–1501	School in Eisenach.
1501– Jan. 1505	Attended the University at Erfurt and received master's degree.
Spring 1505	Beginning of law school at Erfurt.
2 July 1505	Thunderstorm experience; vow to become a monk.
17 July 1505	Admission to the Augustinian monastery in Erfurt.
Spring 1507	Ordained as a priest; began graduate studies in theology at the University of Erfurt.
1508/09	Theological studies and teaching philosophy at Wittenberg.
Nov. 1511 – April 1512	Trip to Rome.
18/19 Oct. 1512	Received doctorate in theology in Wittenberg. Became Johannes von Staupitz's successor for his professorship.
1515–1518	Provincial vicar of his order.
31 Oct. 1517	Beginning of indulgence dispute; 95 Theses; letter to Archbishop Albrecht of Mainz.
March 1518	Theses printed with a Latin explanation and a

	German text outlining central points of critique ("Sermon on Indulgences and Grace").
April 1518	Heidelberg Disputation with a chapter of Augustinian Hermits.
October 1518	Hearing before the Curia's legate, Cardinal Cajetan, at the Imperial Diet of Augsburg. Refusal to recant.
June/July 1519	University of Leipzig disputation against Eck.
Aug./Nov. 1519	Condemnation of Luther by the universities of Cologne and Lowen.
15 June 1520	Pope Leo X issues papal bull threatening excommunication (*Exsurge Domine*).
10 Dec. 1520	Luther publicly burns the papal bull at Wittenberg.
3 Jan. 1521	Luther excommunicated in papal bull (*Decet Romanum Pontificem*).
17–18 April 1521	Refusal to recant before Emperor Charles V at the Diet of Worms.
May 1521	Edict of Worms; sequestered at Wartburg Castle (until Feb. 1522).
9–16 March 1522	Invocavit Sermons; schism of the Wittenberg Reformation; break with Karlstadt.
1524/1525	Controversy with Müntzer; Peasants' War.
13 June 1525	Marriage to Katharina von Bora.
Fall 1525	Conflict with Erasmus (*De Servo Arbitrio*).
1525–1529	Internal reformation conflict with Karlstadt, Zwingli, Oecolampadius, Bucer, etc.
1528/1529	Visits to Saxony; Catechisms.
1534	First "Complete Bible" translation in Wittenberg.
1536	Wittenberg Concord.
1539	Beginning of the Wittenberg edition of Luther's Complete Works.
18 Feb. 1546	Luther dies at Eisleben.
22 Feb. 1546	Luther buried in the Castle Church in Wittenberg.

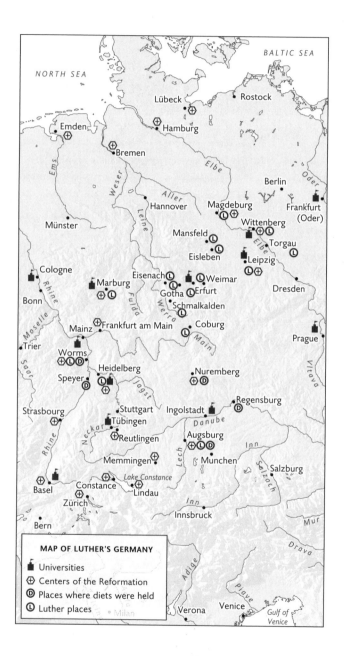

NORTH SEA

BALTIC SEA

Emden

Lübeck   Rostock

Hamburg

Bremen

Ems

Weser

Elbe

Berlin

Oder

Hannover   Magdeburg   Wittenberg   Frankfurt (Oder)

Aller

Leine

Münster

Mansfeld   Torgau

Cologne   Eisenach   Weimar   Leipzig

Rhine   Marburg   Gotha Erfurt   Dresden

Bonn   Fulda Schmalkalden

Moselle   Mainz   Frankfurt am Main   Coburg

Trier   Worms   Prague

Werra

Main

Vltava

Speyer   Heidelberg   Nuremberg

Saar

Strasbourg   Regensburg

Stuttgart   Ingolstadt

Tübingen   Danube

Neckar   Reutlingen   Augsburg   Inn

Jagst   Memmingen   Munchen   Salzburg

Lech

Rhine

Basel   Constance   Lake Constance

Zürich   Lindau   Inn   Salzach

Bern   Innsbruck   Mur

Drava

Adige

Piave

Milan   Verona   Venice   Gulf of Venice

MAP OF LUTHER'S GERMANY

■ Universities
⊕ Centers of the Reformation
Ⓓ Places where diets were held
Ⓛ Luther places

One Person in Two Natures

Martin Luther was a man of opposite extremes, and on many fronts. When he first burst on the public scene, in his attack on the sale of indulgences in 1517, he was just another Augustinian friar, a Bible professor at an obscure university in the middle of Germany. In very short order, however, he rose far above the rank of ordinary mortal in the eyes of thousands. For them he was a direct channel to the transcendent. He embodied radical new convictions about how we might attain—or lose—our salvation; he not only taught new answers but also demanded new commitments on the ultimate question of how God relates to humanity. As a man of extremes, he galvanized extreme reactions, dividing opinion as have few others, before or since.

He was born Martin Luder, his rather unfortunate surname meaning "bait," connoting lout or scoundrel. With his Ninety-Five Theses he became "Eleutherius"—a man set free in God by Christ.[1] It was as this "Luther" that he became famous: hated and honored, reviled as a heretic and lauded as a kind of second Christ. We need not take him (as did some) to be nearly divine, but he certainly was a new-model Christian and undoubtedly a contender for the title Man of the Century. As a man set free in Christ, Luther gave many of his contemporaries reason to rethink what it meant to be a Christian—and, inevitably, to radically question the character of the established church. Many others, however, relished the challenge of answering him in defense of the tried and true Roman Catholic interpretation of faith and life.

Luther was a profoundly inward person whose struggles of soul became legendary. But he was also a public person—in fact, the person through whom publicity as we know it came into being. Like no one before him, he knew how to elicit, mobilize, and deploy public attention and public opinion; the arguments of his age proceeded in, around, and through his name. At the same time, he became publicity's victim, an object of terrible denigration in the service of sometimes dubious purposes. In our terms, Luther was the first media star of history, someone who knew how to use the media revolution of his day—the printing press—while at the same time being consumed by it. Yet, through all this hubbub, he remained above all a quiet, solitary reader, interpreter, and teacher of the Bible at what had previously been an unknown university, newly founded, lacking any tradition, located at the fringe of civilization. By his efforts, however, Wittenberg University experienced its own PR dream, becoming world famous, forever associated with Luther the person and Luther the name.

In Luther the person, two opposite traits were crucial. One was the brooding withdrawal characteristic of the contemplative, the Bible translator, the man ardent in prayer, the spiritual poet, the careful interpreter and composer of texts. But he was just as much a builder, an activist, an open communicator as befitting a preacher and polemicist, a virtuoso of speech who pushed himself onto the public stage. Likewise, Luther was a pronounced introvert and extrovert; he relished intimacy with those close to him and felt compelled to share with total strangers. He was capable of spontaneous trust and the deepest mistrust.

Beneath all these tensions stretched the tension that was most important for his own self-understanding, his historical role, and his historical significance. Luther saw himself standing simultaneously before the face of his God and before the world at the cutting edge of his times. The Luther who prayed and read the Bible also learned how to become a virtuoso litterateur. Conversely, the agitator, fighter, and propagandist always brought that work back to the study of Scripture. He faced two horizons, carried on a twofold speech with God, had two natural ways of being, and in each case one part of the pair made the other one more fruitful. And so he navigated his way—nimbly, adaptably—through a storm of historical challenges, until these finally proved to be too much.

The public Luther proceeded from and was ever sustained by the solitary man who daily bent over the Bible to read it, read it again, and read it a third time, pressing in and drilling down with utter thoroughness and self-torturing intensity. He pounded on the sound of the words in order to pound God's Word out of the human words. For Luther this meditative reading of the Bible was speaking with God. Yet, from that conversation his insight and command of language grew, both compelling and enabling him to go out to the public, for he came to believe that in his day nothing less was at stake than the truth of the Christian faith, which had been lost to the church. He grew convinced that his calling was to declare this sad fact and to raise up the old truth once again.

Thus, the public Luther was not his secondary or "unreal" persona over against the deeply rooted practitioner of prayer and repentance; the two belonged together, inseparably. He developed new spiritual insights as a public person, as a teacher of theology, as a religious author, as someone who was compelled to speak before the public (*coram publico*). Those insights fed back into his understanding of the Bible as a whole and of particular passages in it, into his praying and his relationship with God. In short, as has been tried by too many, we cannot praise, or even adore, Luther the religious genius, "Brother Martinus," or "Father in Faith" while reprimanding or rejecting Luther the agitator, the polemicist, the "betrayer of the peasants," the scourge of heretics, and the enemy of the Jews for his "errors and confusions." Luther was something of all of these, and not exhausted by any of them. His lovable features cannot be balanced against those deserving rejection. They belong together, for Luther remains, in all he said and did, in his greatness and his limitations, a representative of the sixteenth century.

From the start Luther was subjected to different claims and interpretations, and remains so to this day. Some humanists saw him as a fellow fighter for the renewal of literature (*bonae literae*) over against Scholastic theology, and for the liberation of the German nation from the Roman yoke. Some imperial knights welcomed him as a partner in their battle for German freedom against the power of the territorial prince. Some cities saw him as a partner in their struggle for autonomy; some peasants appealed to his authority for their demands for social justice, to abolish the tithe and restore the old godly law. Laypeople invoked Luther's example and teachings to claim their Christian right to voice their religious opinions publicly, as well as their competence to make their own decisions on questions of faith. Borrowing from his exegetical insights, some monks and nuns left their cloisters to claim freedom of conscience against the dictates of their order. These catalytic effects of Luther are not simply misunderstandings (whether productive or problematic) along the course of the Reformation but belong to the heart of his public character.

The cohesiveness of Luther's movement started to dissolve around 1522 when he broke with the so-called Wittenberg movement and its protagonist Andreas Karlstadt. With that, it became painfully clear that one could—in fact, had to—differentiate between what Luther himself thought and what others thought they saw in him, or projected onto him. The subsequent history of the Reformation, with its divergence into separate theological parties and ecclesiastical networks, including the Reformed and Anabaptist, made this clarification even more important.

This tension over the public Luther has been perpetuated in the polarity that later interpreters have drawn between the young pioneering "progressive" and the older, orthodox "conservative." As for Luther himself, however, none of the discontinuities in his life or in the many developments that came along over the years, the lot of it inseparably fused with the history of his time, altered the defining dialectic of his life. The "young" as well as the "old" Luther lived at once completely in his relationship to God and completely in public: *coram Deo* and *coram hominibus*. He remained always a man of prayer and a man of action.

So long as Luther lived, he could respond to the appraisals and claims that others imposed on him. He did so selectively and strategically. He entered controversies only when he could articulate his position clearly, and remained in them only as long as it took him to do so; once he had "established the truth," he assumed that the purpose of the dispute had been served and left it alone. The Word of God, he believed, was efficacious to this end; theological opponents thus dispatched needed no further engagement from him.

But Luther's historical significance went well beyond his involvement with such controversies and the daily business of the Reformation. He never lost sight of his greater literary projects, which ranged from publishing his postils,[2] to publishing his catechisms and Bible commentaries, to printing his translation of the Bible. Persistently, step by step, he followed through on these projects, working day and night. Somehow he kept himself from being consumed by the many duties in which he found himself—and in which he involved himself. Rather, his tasks as professor and preacher imposed an outward organization that enabled him to continue his work on biblical interpretation. This combination of discipline and latitude enabled him to complete pressing literary tasks without interruption. In short, Luther the writer was both the day-by-day pamphleteer and the patient, careful, steady Bible exegete and translator who wanted to create works of lasting significance.

Luther's death brought no end to the many interpretations and appraisals of him made by friend and foe alike. In the Lutheran branch of Protestantism, both the man and the Reformation he was deemed to have providentially birthed became fixed reference points for building and maintaining identity. Next to the Bible, these points were at one and the same time the most stable and the most susceptible to interpretation, but vital for giving the church direction. At the opposite pole, critics of Lutheranism—or of Christianity in general—found in Luther their most august target.

In subsequent Protestant history, leaders at every stage and phase sought to find some sort of positive connection with him. That is, though he was not accorded a rank or authority on a par with the Bible, all invoked him to legitimate their particular teachings and their idea of the Reformation's true meaning. To Lutheran confessionalists he was a divinely ordained interpreter of the Bible, the doctor of the church without equal. They developed a system of summarizing Luther's doctrines in short teachable sentences that students were to recite and reflect upon, in the hopes of thus harvesting his spiritual legacy for the present.

The practice of using Luther strategically began with the Pietists, who designated Luther's "two natures" as two stages of development. Their own ideas for church reform they grounded in the "young" pioneer who had liberated the laity by insisting on the priesthood of all believers. Simultaneously they marginalized the old, intransigent Luther who had defended church offices and orthodoxy. This sometimes openly selective handling of the Reformer's theology, which became customary from the seventeenth century on, naturally did not diminish any party's high esteem for his merits. The Enlightenment could claim him as an early apostle of the freedom of conscience; German patriots could lift him up as a standard-bearer of German nationality; Protestant liberals retrospectively used his voice to legitimate the freedom of faith, all the while critically adjusting the premodern features of his theology on the points of anthropology, worldview, and scriptural understanding. At the hands of nationalist Protestants, folk theologians, and Nazi ideologues, a pure German, anti-Western, or anti-Semitic Luther became the gauge of his conformity to the time, and immersed him so deeply in the maelstrom of spiritual barbarism as to bring down Thomas Mann's stinging indictment of him in 1945 as the "stiff-necked barbarian of God."

But all these miss the historical person of Luther. So do all the other more or less positive judgments pronounced upon the interpretations of Luther that have accumulated in four hundred years of historical interpretation. That Luther today remains the best-known and most esteemed figure of German history—indeed, he is counted as "our best" according to the title of a recent German telecast—is not only because of regular Luther commemorations and tourist-culture marketability, but also because he satisfies a longing for a memory of a cultural point in German history that predates 1933. From all this older history, Luther is the German about whom we know the most.

Luther's character, as it is traced in this book, derived

from one simple observation: Luther lived wholly in the present and wholly in his faith. In his mind the two did not stand detached from each other. On the contrary, Luther's faith was shaped by the experiences of his era, while that faith simultaneously opened up those experiences and disclosed their meaning. As little as Luther's person can be understood outside of the historical relationships in which he lived, he was so much more than the sum of those relationships.

Thus, on the one hand Luther represents a person who was thoroughly stamped by his historical ambience; on the other hand, he knew himself to be completely determined and carried along by the immediate working of God. In Luther, theology and biography, faith and experience, contemplation and action were inseparable, and far more interwoven than was true for most of his theological contemporaries. These close correlations define Luther's particular quality and significance. For that reason the search for the historical Luther has to deal at once with his life *and* his faith, his time *and* his God, his self-consciousness *and* the judgments made of him—all as one package of dynamic relationships. By his own self-appraisal his life seemed hopelessly fragmented; to his eyes of faith it was wholly fulfilled and certain. By the standards of the day his life took place far from the political and cultural centers of power. Yet it changed the Western Church, and thereby the world, as has seldom happened before, or since.

CHAPTER ONE

The Search for Martin Luther

Because countless thinkers have interpreted Martin Luther and have painted wildly different portraits of him, the best place to begin to understand Luther is with his self-perception. Who did Martin Luther think he was?

Luther spoke and wrote about himself very often and in very different formats—in table talk and letters to intimate friends, but also in sermons and works addressed to the general public. It would be difficult to name a contemporary or predecessor, at least among theologians, who talked about himself as frequently as he. Moreover, Luther *needed* to talk about himself, both because of the intense and unparalleled scrutiny to which he was subjected, and because of the close relationship between his person and his theology.

In Luther we see an oscillation between the most extreme opposites imaginable: the highest self-certainty and the deepest sense of unworthiness, lighthearted confidence and dark self-accusation. Two cultural trends were clearly at work here: from the medieval monastic tradition he inherited a tendency toward scrupulous self-denial, and from recently risen humanism he passed along an affirmation of people and their possibilities. Luther combined these into a rich tension that corresponded to his understanding of what it means to be a Christian.

And that—the simple conviction that, at bottom, he was

"a Christian"—constitutes the central theme that runs across all of Luther's modes and moments of self-interpretation. He put it precisely in his 1525 polemic against Erasmus: "I have nothing and am nothing, except that I can almost boast to be a Christian" (*Ego vero nihil habeo et sum, nisi quod Christianum esse me prope glorier*).[1] Long personal experience honed the central axiom of his theological anthropology to a sharp edge: strive as we might with all our strength of will, in the eyes of God we can accomplish nothing. And so his last written statement, composed on February 16, 1546, just two days before his death, aptly closed with these words: "We are beggars, *hoc est verum* [that is true]."[2] That also held for human understanding, above all with regard to Scripture: we cannot understand it without the trials of experience and the sustaining support of the Holy Spirit, which we cannot control. In short, the central feature of Luther's self-understanding was his complete dependence on faith alone for the assured grace of God.

On his public side, he staked his claim to credibility solely on the conviction that the knowledge of Christ and his gospel had been imparted to him and spread through him. His testament of 1542 put it this way: "I ask of every man . . . that he would allow me to be the person which in truth I am, namely, a public figure known both in heaven and on earth, as well as in hell, bearing respect or authority enough that one can trust or believe me more than any notary. For God, the father of all mercies, entrusted to me, a condemned, poor, unworthy, and miserable sinner, the gospel of his dear Son and made me faithful and truthful, and has up to now preserved and grounded me in it, so that many in the world have accepted it through me and hold me to be a teacher of the truth, without regard for the pope's ban and the anger of emperor, kings, princes, clerics, yes, of all the devils."[3] Luther's self-concept held steadfast simply because he applied to himself the basic insight of his faith, namely, that God's provision of grace and freedom to the sinner is not based on the worthiness of the human being but on undeserved mercy alone. His confession of sin was inseparably interwoven with his certainty of justification; only God could overcome our distance from God, indeed, our enmity for God. This was the theological basis for his many tension-packed, dialectical self-descriptions.

We can see this already in the first act that spread his name beyond the narrow confines of the university, in his change of surname from Luder to Luther at the start of the indulgences controversy. The first time he clearly used his new name was in a letter of October 31, 1517, to Archbishop Albrecht of Mainz, the authority responsible for the sale of indulgences in that part of Germany. The letter demanded that the high-pressure sales campaign cease at once, and was accompanied by a copy of the Ninety-Five Theses. It was a bold action reflecting the self-confidence of a man who had been completely set free in the bond of Christ. In the Greek and Latin form of his new name, Eleutherius, "the free one," Martin Luder saw an etymological verification of the secret that God had hidden in his family name. In a letter to his friend Johannes Lang, on November 11, 1517, he embellished his signature accordingly: "Brother Martinus Eleutherius, yes, all too much a servant and captive, Augustinian at Wittenberg."[4] From then on he pointedly reiterated this characteristic dialectic: from God's point of view, Luther knew himself to be righteous and free; from his own perspective, he was a captive of sin and an unworthy servant.

His name change and all that it signified bore unmistakable parallels to self-references made by the apostle Paul, another name-changer. In Galatians 1:12, a verse Luther could well have claimed as his own, Paul declared that he had received the gospel "not from man, but from heaven alone through our Lord Jesus Christ."[5] Luther could identify his fight against the "papists" with the apostle's fight against his Judaizing opponents. As Paul boasted of his "weakness" to the Corinthians[6] (Luther detected some "holy pride"[7] on the apostle's part here), so Luther militantly asserted his authority as an "unworthy evangelist"[8] who nonetheless was more "learned in scripture" than "all the Sophists and Papists."[9] Even if Luther did not claim personal inspiration in the sense of having received an immediate revelation ("I do not claim to be a prophet"),[10] he most certainly did claim knowledge of the truth as mediated by the strength of the biblical word and a divine mandate to spread it, for "even if I am not a prophet, as far as I am concerned I am sure that the Word of God is with me and not with them [his 'papist' opponents], for I have the Scriptures on my side and they have only their own doctrine."[11] But this certainty was pierced by self-doubt whenever he pondered the question of how he could be right as a single person against the authority of the pope's church and all the weight of interpretive tradition in understanding the Christian faith: "How often did my heart quail and reproach me with their [i.e., 'the papists'] single strongest argument: 'You alone are wise? Can it be that all the others are in error and have been for so long a time?'"[12]

At the heart of Luther's dialectical self-understanding were the trials of faith that swelled up, his whole life long, in episodes of *Anfechtungen*, "torment." From biblical examples he was convinced that God had sustained the church since creation through solitary witnesses to the truth: through patriarchs like Adam, Abraham, and perhaps Noah; through Old Testament prophets like Isaiah and Daniel; and finally through teachers of the church like Augustine, Ambrose, and Bernard of Clairvaux. And so also he sometimes seems to have understood himself as a kind of final witness before the apocalyptic last days, and to that extent as an "end-time prophet."[13] Bit by bit he heard of prophecies of a "hermit" who would attack the papacy of Leo X[14] or, in 1516, of someone who would destroy monasticism.[15] These prophecies could hardly have left him unaffected since they were all about him and were passed along by some of his busy epigones. The dynamic success of the "run of the gospel" in the Reformation of the early 1520s against all attempts to hinder it validated his sense of divine calling: "But God has opened my mouth and bidden me to speak, and he supports me mightily. The more they rage against me, the more he strengthens and extends my cause—without any help or advice from me—as if he were laughing and holding their rage in derision. . . . Therefore, I will speak (as Isaiah says) and not keep silent as long as I live."[16] Luther's claims likely exceeded those of any ancient or medieval theologian. He declared himself to be a God-"ordained" preacher for the "German nation,"[17] indeed, a "prophet of the Germans."[18] In deciding for or against him, people were determining their relationship with Christ;[19] his cause was the cause of God;[20] through him Christ would kill the papacy.[21] He was presenting no "new" teaching, only the core of the "old" biblical proclamation, recovering it for the first time in centuries. Luther lived in the certainty that God would bear witness at the last judgment that he had taught well.[22]

Luther's self-consciousness of being a teacher of the true church—one instructed in, and indeed, compelled to that role by Scripture—only grew after he was declared a heretic by the "pope's church." His doctorate in theology was particularly important for him at the start of his altercation with Scholastic theology and the system of penance and indulgences. The office of professor of theology bore with it—in good "medieval" fashion, and conveyed by full apostolic authority[23]—the church's own mandate that he defend orthodoxy and fight against every teaching that was in error.

Even more, via his university position under Augustinian auspices, the church had given him the right to exercise his own theological judgment in carrying out this duty.

Thus, Luther participated in the life of his community as the holder of an office; he "was not only a fool, but also a sworn doctor of Holy Scripture."[24] He was simply taking a stand for the truth of the gospel as required by his "conscience, oath, and duty, and as a poor teacher of the Holy Scripture."[25] After he had been "robbed of his title" by papal excommunication and the imperial ban,[26] other self-descriptions moved into the foreground, especially "Ecclesiastes" ("Preacher") and "Evangelist." But Luther did not relinquish his doctoral title, which would have amounted to accepting his condemnation as a heretic. Indeed, in arguments with opponents both inside and outside of Reformation ranks,[27] he used his degree to bolster his right to teach.

Even though (as he saw it in retrospect) he had first opposed accepting that title with all its attendant obligations, his acquiescence on this point proved to be the source and ground of the further theological development that eventually brought him to oppose the pope's church: "However, I, Doctor Martinus, have been called to this work and was compelled to become a doctor, without any initiative of my own, but out of pure obedience. Then I had to accept the office of doctor and swear a vow to my most dearly beloved Holy Scriptures that I would preach and teach them faithfully and purely. While engaged in this kind of teaching, the papacy crossed my path and tried to hinder me in it."[28] Luther's claim that ecclesiastical opposition prevented him from fulfilling his ecclesiastical obligation ran as a continuous theme through every stage of his life from the moment he graduated with his doctorate in October 1512. In calling himself "an ecclesiast by God's grace" or "an evangelist by God's grace,"[29] Luther the heretic asserted in the most provocative way imaginable that everything he had to say proceeded simply "on the prompting . . . of the Spirit"[30] and that Christ "is the master of my teaching and would be the witness on the last day that it is not mine but his pure gospel."[31]

Luther's conviction of the truth, like his self-understanding, rested theologically on the elementary fact that he was, "however unworthy, a baptized Christian."[32] From that core of personal identity, grounded not in himself but in God or Christ, he gained the flexibility to manage the historical individual Martin Luther. Thus he could imitate the apostle's self-boasting (in 2 Cor. 11:2–3) in describing himself as "a doctor over all the doctors of the whole papacy,"[33] yet call himself "the stinking bag of worms" whose "wretched name," that is, "Lutheran," the "children of Christ" should absolutely not adopt for themselves.[34] That this Pauline dialectic of freedom and servanthood in Christ had no model in the standard value-system of medieval Christianity—though it may have had a parallel in cultural history to the figure of the fool[35]—accounts for much of the great interest taken in his person.

Luther's self-concept also drew off the perceptions and assessments of sympathetic contemporaries. Of this company, the furthest removed from his driving passion were probably the humanists in the circle of Erasmus. They thought they had common cause with him because they cast his fight for the gospel in light of their own struggle for the renewal of literature (*bonae literae*); likewise, they opposed Scholastic theology and the "superstitious" abuses of the church. But however important they were for the early spread of Lutheran ideas and texts, the Erasmians' theological foundation proved to be very different from Luther's, and the two sides brusquely separated after 1520.

His long-lasting allies favored him with elevated titles.

He was a "man" or "servant" of God, a chosen instrument of Christ. To Wolfgang F. Capito, a native of Basel, preacher at Münster, and professor of theology, he was a prophet in the line of Daniel; so Capito stated in publishing the earliest collection of Luther texts in the fall of 1518.[36] Ulrich Zwingli, the preacher and reformer from Zürich, thought him to be "Elijah" instead, a name that Melanchthon would especially favor. The title of Elijah bore apocalyptic associations and accordingly enjoyed considerable popularity at the beginning of the Reformation. It also sealed an enduring and compelling Lutheran interpretation of the Wittenberg reformer's place in salvation history. On this account, when the Antichrist appears, God will send back the prophet Elijah (who had not died but had been taken up into heaven)[37] to warn and comfort hard-pressed Christians with the announcement of the Lord's imminent return. A pamphlet probably dating from 1521, *On the Christ-Forming Teaching of Luther*, laid out this case with the enthusiasm kindled by Luther's recent defiant stand at the Diet of Worms. It came from the pen of one Michael Stifel, a fellow Augustinian friar and an early follower of Luther, and testified: "After deciphering the signs stipulated in the Bible for the end of the world, by the grace of God I cannot but hold with Martin Luther that that very time is drawing nigh in which the Antichrist will lead the deceitful persecution of the truth of God. I believe that this man was sent to us by God, ordained and quickened with the fervor of the spirit of Elijah to discover and open the secret, subtle betrayal of the Antichrist, his messengers, and servants." Although Luther would have certainly distanced himself from the idea that Elijah would "return,"[38] he never seems to have contradicted having the name applied to himself.[39] That it was God and not, as the "papists" believed, he himself who had set afoot the radical changes at work in the world was for Luther an insight that only could be won by faith.[40]

One of the most successful pamphlets, *The Passion of Doctor Martin Luther*, cast Luther's confrontation at the Diet of Worms in artful imitation of the passion of Christ. This elevated him in salvation history to being the standard by which one's relationship to Christ would be determined. This Christ-Luther parallel had a certain hold on Luther himself in the epochal years 1517–1521.[41] The parallel, to be sure, did not so much claim soteriological significance for Luther himself as it evoked the familiar devotional trope of the imitation of Christ.[42] Still, in light of the looming end of the world, and in light of Christ's representing himself in Luther's teaching, one's decision concerning Luther amounted to one's decision about Christ. This cult of Luther furnished Rome's loyalists with welcome evidence for the abject character of his heresy.

The acute public interest in Luther was reflected in an extensive production of woodcuts and copper engravings available already before the showdown at Worms. It was highly unusual to see portrait-like depictions of a man belonging to a religious order thus disseminated; evidently it filled people's craving to know the facial features of the famous Bible professor and accused heretic. Lucas Cranach the Elder, a friend of Luther and a busy artist at the court of Elector Frederick of Saxony, proved to be an extraordinarily productive creator of different Luther images, which were often developed in close tandem with court politics. The most popular image, often placed into niches, cast Luther in the traditional pose of a saint with Bible in hand, looking up toward heaven. Sometimes Cranach cast Luther as the Augustinian friar, now meditative, now ready to speak. Then the pose shifted to a monumental half-portrait, in the mode of heroic typology, of Luther the man of learning. Then again he was the noble upholder of law and order, the man with the beard who had ended the Wittenberg Disturbances.

Now he was a steadfast church father with clear, penetrating gaze; now a married man and solid citizen. No figure of early modern German history was visualized so often, in so many forms, and in such different media as Martin Luther.

Early on in the Reformation Luther was cast as "the Man of God" with a dove, a bearer of the Holy Spirit for the last days. Reports that people offered religious devotion before these pictures seem to be credible; for many this monk-become-media-star was a new saint. We cannot know whether Luther himself had any substantial influence on the ways he was depicted, but he did not hinder the trade—and perhaps could not have done so even if he wanted to. He always insisted that the "authentic" expression of his "spiritual picture" was in his writings. To him, the interest taken in his person only served to further spread the gospel. For that cause he stood, and with his success in that cause Luther saw the cause of Christ being borne out by God's mighty action in history. Yet that reality was only recognizable by faith. Any portrayal that made him more than human he turned instead into a reminder that he was but a sinner made free in Christ. This guided him, amid all his rich and manifold experience in the everyday world, back to the end of time.

CHAPTER TWO

Living in the Reformation of God

God's Reformation

Luther had plenty of company in believing that the church needed a basic reformation (*reformatio*), and in thinking that it would not come from the pope, or from a host of cardinals. Not even the whole world could bring it about. God alone could do it. As Luther put it: "The timing of this reformation (*tempus autem huius reformationes*) is known by God alone, who created the times."[1]

Until then, what mattered was to expose open and evident abuses, like those surrounding the sale of indulgences. In this Luther himself (or as he saw it, the Word of God proclaimed through him) was but an "actor." In any case, such exposés and more certainly took place in what Luther called the "victory run of the gospel," the broad and rapid spread of the Reformation movement between the Leipzig Disputation in the summer of 1519 and the Diet of Worms in spring 1521.

In the middle of this period, during 1520, Luther sharpened his accusations: it had become evident that the Roman pope was the Antichrist and that the time of the God-ordained reformation had begun. In fact, this was the end-time reformation, the moment when the heavenly Lord of history would restore his church in accordance with the

Gospels and his will, one last time before judgment day. All the remaining time of the world, whether it be one, two, or three human ages, was only more of the "last times."

From the mid-1520s on, the reformation of the church was gradually realized under the protection of Protestant territorial lords and city magistrates. However, that dimmed the universal expectation of its extension into a comprehensive reformation of the entire church. Undoubtedly, the reformation that did occur accomplished goals that Luther considered to be objectively justified. In 1537, during a controversy over the pope's refusal to call a church council, Luther retorted: "For our part—our church . . . [having been] enlightened and equipped by the grace of God with the pure Word and the right use of the sacraments, and with the knowledge of all kinds of stands and right works—we ask for no council and neither hope nor expect that much good will come from one."[2] Luther was convinced that with "his Gospel" he had "reformed more"[3] than the pope's church could have done with five councils. With its spread and its accord with the gospel, the genuine achievement of the Reformation in the city and territorial churches that had become evangelical under his influence counted for the later Luther as the same reformation the younger Luther, at the start of his controversy with the Church of Rome, had awaited as the work of God.

That the Reformation had not visibly changed the entire *orbis christianum* out to the four corners of the Christian world did not count against its truth and legitimacy, in Luther's mind. Ultimately it did not matter, because everything was grounded in God's secret plan for history. Running across Luther's whole life was the expectation that the macrohistorical reformation at the end of time would get its start and take its concrete formation in the microhistorical, everyday processes by which churches were converted to the genuine gospel. What lay beyond that might seem fleeting in light of the nearness of the end, but it was important to secure the vital thing: the right proclamation of the Word and administration of the sacraments. A historicization of the reformation as an epoch in an ongoing history, whose future is still to be written, lay as far beyond his mental horizon as did the conception of a church permanently reforming itself.

Luther's life divides between a more or less hidden early phase and a later period that is better known because of the abundant sources available from the time. In 1517, when the transition from the first to the second period took place, Luther was already thirty-four years old; although he spoke of it otherwise, he was no longer a "young" man by the standards of the time. He had been professor of theology at the University of Wittenberg for five years (and that would remain his vocational base to his death) and had worn the robe of the Augustinian Order for twelve. Filling in the contours of his earlier life depends significantly on information he dispensed years later, when he looked back and talked of his childhood and youth, as well as his years in the monastery and the start of his controversy with the church. Such information certainly needs to be used critically, but in any case we can conclude that his early circumstances offer few if any plausible clues to explain his later development. On the one hand this is a consequence of the meager state of the sources; on the other, it is based on the central feature of his development—he was driven by his relationship with God.

Childhood and Youth

Martin was born on November 10, 1483, in Eisleben and baptized the next day with the name of that day's patron saint. He was the first or second son of Margarete née Lindemann (died June 30, 1531), from a family in Eisenach, and Hans Luder (died May 29, 1530), the son of a Thuringian farmer. Hans had taken up copper mining, a growing branch of the economy at the time, and in 1484 moved the family to the city of Mansfeld. There he worked himself up from a simple pick man to become a smelting master and the co-owner of several mining enterprises. This was prosperity enough to provide Martin with an education carefully directed toward a higher career. Although Luther's home and schooling ran normally by the standards of the day, Martin later remembered them as excessively harsh, and sought to avoid the same in bringing up his own children. Martin seems to have had eight siblings, of whom four survived to adulthood: his brother Jacob, with whom he was especially close, and three sisters. The growing Luder family and the struggle to establish themselves in business and society required the parents to exercise strict discipline over spending and nurture, which hardly gave so sensitive and fearful a boy as Martin a warm and protective home.

Luther learned about religion from the typical spectrum of church life in a small city. There were saints in colorful profusion to be adored, especially Mary and her mother, Saint Anne, part of the "Holy Family" valued by the good burghers of the city. There were pilgrimages, indulgences, and devotional exercises sponsored by various religious foundations. There were regular masses that applied the sacramental sacrifice of the Redeemer to the healing of souls, whether for a single donor or for pious societies associating themselves in confraternities. All this and much more: mother Margarete Luder's well-attested fear of witches was also part of the scene. The relationship of parents to children in Martin's family was thus determined by an ultimately religious sense of bonds and connections, as became painfully clear when Luther's father invoked the commandment about honoring one's mother and father when his son announced his "unacceptable" decision to become a monk.

Between 1490 and 1497 Luther probably attended the Mansfeld city school; thereafter, he spent a year in Magdeburg, the largest city in north-central Germany, probably at the grammar school attached to the cathedral. Also in attendance was Hans Reineck, the son of another Mansfeld burgher, who later became a foundry master in his hometown and one of Martin's longtime contacts. Several other acquaintances from this Magdeburg period, especially the future mayor, Claus Storm, would become important for the development of the Reformation in this metropolis on the Elbe River.

However strategic Magdeburg might have been, Luther's move in spring 1498 to the school connected to St. George's church in Eisenach opened up a much happier school experience. The rector of the school, Luther later recalled, would remove his biretta upon entering the classroom out of respect for the pupils, among whom sat future mayors, chancellors, and doctors.[4] Some of his mother's relatives lived in Eisenach as well, representing a family tradition that esteemed academic learning. Martin was welcomed in the home of a family friend, Hans Schalbe, a future mayor of Eisenach. Luther always gratefully remembered the close ties between the burgher families of Shalbe and Cotta and the devoted teaching staff (*collegium*) of local Franciscans. The vicar at the Foundation of Mary in Eisenach, Johannes Braun, a priest probably already in his fifties during Luther's schooling there, proved to be a fatherly friend who remained in contact with him during his further studies at Erfurt and Wittenberg. Braun was the first church person we know of in Luther's life who left a deep and lasting impression on him.

At the end of his school years Luther would have been able to read, write, and speak Latin; show competence in the basic rhetoric of the *ars epistolandi*, the art of letter writing; and have some knowledge of music theory, which was customarily taught as part of mathematics. Given the pupils' regular participation in planning worship services, we can also assume he was well versed in singing and liturgy. Luther's strong development as a student of the liberal arts at the University of Erfurt attests to the good grounding he had received amid the advantageous milieu of Eisenach.

University Life

Luther's decision to take up university studies at Erfurt, in the summer of 1501, fit in well with the Lindemann family tradition of his mother and with his positive experience at Eisenach. In the medieval university system, students would take preparatory work in the seven liberal arts before proceeding, if they wished, to graduate study in one of the three higher faculties: theology, law, or medicine. The first stage, which culminated in a baccalaureate degree, required at least three semesters of work in grammar, logic, and natural philosophy, all oriented to the pertinent works of Aristotle. Most students left after completing those exams. A master's degree required at least four years of schooling, which included study of geometry, arithmetic, astronomy, metaphysics, and moral philosophy (comprising politics, economics, and ethics). The curriculum was designed to convey the church's integrated world of knowledge with a specialized logical vocabulary, thus drilling students in the basic techniques of effective argumentation and debate. Despite his later disparagements of the contemporary university and its guiding star, Aristotle, this training provided Luther with well-honed skills that would prove unendingly useful in the many roles of his long career.

The liberal arts faculty of the University of Erfurt was dominated by the nominalist philosophy of William of Ockham, the *via moderna* (modern way) in Scholasticism. It would play a central role in Luther's entire intellectual development, not least in logic. Nominalism differed from the *via antiqua* (old way) that was associated above all with the work of Thomas Aquinas. Thomas's "realism" assumed that general concepts or categories (universals) were real, and derived the reality of concrete individual things from those universals. The nominalist *via moderna* proceeded in the opposite direction. Reality existed only in individual things, and universals were only categories in the human mind that were established by certain naming (*nomen*) conventions; that is, we agree to call particular things that share some common attributes by a certain name. This antispeculative, experience-oriented approach, as Luther encountered it at Erfurt in the widely respected Professors Jodocus Trutfetter (died 1519) and Bartholomew Arnoldi von Usingen (died 1532), helped him develop a keener awareness for the concrete meanings of words and their context. These tendencies coincided with the contemporary endeavors of some humanists to develop a more elegant Latin style. A decidedly anti-Scholastic humanism, of the sort that Luther's student friend Crotus Rubeanus would later develop, did not yet exist during his time at Erfurt, so that we can say that the early-humanist influence on Luther went little beyond knowing a few Latin authors and an increased sensitivity to how Latin was expressed.

Everyday life for a student like Luther followed an order quite similar to that of a monk. Everybody roomed, boarded, and studied together. All were under the command of the rector, a master of the liberal arts faculty, who supervised their work discipline, prescribed their dress, and enforced their obligation to speak Latin. He regulated their dormitories, study rooms, and alcohol consumption, and enforced the prohibition of any contact with the opposite sex. The students might have been excused for thinking that they were indeed living in a monastery.

Luther proceeded through his studies without interruption and, it seems, with growing success. In the fall of 1502 he completed the baccalaureate exam, ranking thirtieth in a class of fifty-seven; in January 1505 he passed the master's exam as the second of seventeen candidates. The success of "Master Martin," whom his father now addressed respectfully with the formal "you" (in German, no longer *du* but *Sie*), seemed to justify the exorbitant investment made in his education.[5] There is nothing to indicate that the student Martinus was not at the same time that "dashing, happy, and young fellow" whom Crotus Rubeanus remembered, fond of comradery and good on the lute. It might well be that already in this premonastery period Luther suffered episodes of torment (*Anfechtungen*) and religious self-doubt. But if he did not allow his mates to look into his heart, we cannot either at this distance in time. What we can know is that, in taking up the study of law in the summer term of 1505 and the undergraduate teaching obligations it entailed, he was following the projected career plan that his parents had long envisioned for their son.

Into the Monastery

Luther's motives for entering the monastery are necessarily difficult to reconstruct. The lightning bolt that nearly struck him on July 2, 1505, was the external reason. This happened near the village of Stotternheim, six kilometers from Erfurt, on Luther's return from a midterm visit to his parents at Mansfeld. The storm triggered his fear of death and probably did induce his proverbial vow, "Help me, Saint Anne, I will become a monk."[6]

But what were the internal conditions that not only provoked this pledge but also pressed him to honor it despite everyone's counsel to the contrary? No doubt his piety, first of all, played a role, but then too did his need to make a decision about his vocational and personal future. This question had grown into something of a crisis. Nothing indicates that a life in the law was part of what this twenty-one-year-old had envisioned for himself. More urgent, and probably the reason for his unusual visit home in the middle of the semester, was the marriage plan concocted by his father, advantageous from his point of view but definitely not welcomed by the son.[7] The plague that raged through Erfurt in 1505 might well have confronted Luther pointedly with the big questions about the meaning of life and salvation. In that context, to experience the transcendent power of God in a terrifying moment in nature brought Luther to see the vulnerability of his own life very close up.

In short, he was converted by fear and terror, as was Paul on the road to Damascus.[8] It seemed plausible that the lightning bolt of the Lord of life and death did not hit and annihilate him owing to the intercession of Saint Anne, the mother of Mary, whom he had invoked to pray for him. In the face of the punishing God who had descended so directly into Luther's life, such a vow had to be kept. Surrendering his life to the God who had made an attempt on that life might have seemed a fitting exchange; and in the religious culture of the day, surrendering one's life meant becoming a monk.

So the interplay between Luther's inner disposition and the storm at Stotternheim, of his experience of helplessness and its religious interpretation, made this into a life-changing moment. Even after long talks with his friends in Erfurt, and registering the deep dismay of his father, Luther held fast to the binding nature of his vow against all objections. He formally marked his departure from the world two weeks later when, accompanied by his friends on the morning of July 17, 1505, he disappeared behind the walls of the Augustinian monastery at Erfurt with the solemn words: "Today you see me and never more!"[9] With that he left his former existence in what was probably the first life decision he had made on his own. His step issued from a confrontation with the annihilating judgment of an aggressive, almighty God. Into the church Luther carried his despair over his former life and his hope for a new one.

Monk and Professor

Luther's choice of the strict (or "observant") mendicant order of Augustinian friars can be explained by the order's good reputation in Erfurt and by the mesh of its academic program with his previous education. He probably knew of the brothers by their activities, such as preaching, in and around the city and university. After a one-year novitiate, in which he had to learn the rules and routine of monastery living, he took the solemn vows that obligated him to a lifelong observance of poverty, chastity, and obedience. During his novitiate, and on his own initiative, he took up an intensive study of the Bible that stayed with him for the rest of his life. Already he was surpassing the normal round of confession, self-examination, private prayer, and frequent worship typical of monastic life. After taking his vows, Luther was directed by his prior to prepare himself for consecration as a priest. He immersed himself in the canon of the Mass as interpreted by the late nominalist Gabriel Biel (died 1495) and in the practice of confession as summarized by Angelus de Clavasio (died 1495), a book he would commit to the flames fifteen years later along with copies of the canon law and the bull threatening his excommunication. He was consecrated as a priest on May 3, 1507, on which occasion he celebrated his first Mass (the *Primiz*) in the presence of his father, who had arrived with a great entourage and gave a gift of twenty gulden to the monastery.

Luther's early years in the cloister seem to have revolved around a fundamental tension between the trust with which his superiors observed his development and his own sentiments of deep inadequacy that flowed from his unceasing self-examination. The latter was accompanied by episodes of despair that drove him to seek the help of the sacrament of confession again and again, over and above the many times it was offered in the monastery's usual round. This ferment of religious unrest took theological form in his questions about how we can gain certainty about God and grace. The earnestness of monastic life, whose daily obligations entailed never-ending repentance, laid the background and constituted fertile soil for questions that Luther now incessantly sought to answer from the Bible.

The same year he was consecrated as a priest, his Augustinian superiors directed him to begin graduate studies in theology at the University of Erfurt. The road to the doctorate had several well-defined steps. First came a baccalaureate exam on the Bible, in which he had to give a cursory explanation of one book from the Old Testament and one book from the New.[10] Then, an exam in two parts on the most important medieval textbook in dogmatics, the *Sentences* of Peter Lombard (died 1160): first on books 1 and 2, then on 3 and 4.[11] Luther proceeded through them all without interruption but was not able to finish his examination before he left for Wittenberg in summer 1511.

For the 1508–1509 academic year, he was assigned to teach moral philosophy at Wittenberg while continuing his theological studies. Besides the Scholastic theology he absorbed in Ockham's nominalist tradition, Luther was also influenced during these years by mystical devotional texts mediated through his reading of Jean Gerson, Bernard of Clairvaux, and Bonaventure. The anonymously authored mystical tract *The German Theology* was the first work he saw through the press, a partial edition in 1516 and a complete text in 1518. From it, he confessed, he had "learned more . . . [about] what God, Christ, the human being, and all things meant" than from all other books "next to the Bible and Saint Augustine."[12] The special influence of Augustine can be detected already from the time he taught the *Sentences* (Erfurt, Spring 1510) and from his further commentary on Peter Lombard.[13]

His teaching was interrupted by the trip Luther made to Rome from fall 1511 to spring 1512. He took it, accompanied by a fellow Augustinian, to try to solve a political problem roiling the order. At issue was the independent standing of the seven "observant" Augustinian monasteries that were especially strict in keeping the rules of the order. Johannes von Staupitz, who taught Bible at Wittenberg from 1502 on, was also vicar-general of the Augustinians' observant congregations in middle and north Germany and was pressing for an administrative merger of them with the nonobservant houses. Some of the observant abbeys, among them Luther's at Erfurt, feared that such a merger would dilute the rigor of their discipline, so Luther's assignment seemed to be to address the protest of the observant abbeys before the head of the order in Rome. Getting there involved traveling weeks on foot in the cold of winter and took on the character of a pilgrimage.

Besides his lobbying, Luther used his four weeks' stay in the holy city of Western Christianity to accumulate as many spiritual merits as possible for himself and for deceased members of his family, through a busy round of confessions, pilgrimages to the graves of martyrs, fasts, and celebrating a Mass himself. In the process the pious German monk saw much to dismay him—the rote reading of the Mass by the Italian priests and the worldly pomp displayed by church dignitaries. Even if this experience did not cause Luther's eventual alienation from the pope's church, once that break had occurred, his month in Rome certainly offered him a rich repertoire to illustrate the papacy's terrible decadence.

As for his official mission, the two friars from Saxony achieved nothing. Yet this did not sour Luther's relationship with Staupitz, to whom he had become close spiritually and theologically during his first term at Wittenberg in 1508–1509. Perhaps the two came to agreement on the matter.

According to Luther's later reflections, Staupitz seems to have played a key role in Luther's theological development. He especially countered Luther's existential fear of a wrathful God with the conviction, deeply anchored in monastic spirituality, that the punishments of a righteous God were sent to bring about the salvation of the sinner. He pointed particularly to the suffering Christ, whose very rejection revealed his election by God. It was to Staupitz's urging that Luther's final step at the Wittenberg cloister, in fall 1511, has to be ascribed. Staupitz saw in this sincere brother, who was equipped with such extraordinary insights into the Bible, a fitting successor for the professorship he himself had held since the founding of the university. When he acquired the official degree of doctor of theology in ceremonies on October 18–19, 1512, Luther was authorized for *lectio, disputatio,* and *praedicatio*—lecturing, disputations, and preaching—with all the rights and privileges pertaining thereto. That is, he was licensed to conduct independent theological teaching.

Luther's was a regular chair of theology, but he diverged

from contemporary practice by using it exclusively to lecture on the Bible. He lectured on the New Testament for only four and a half of the thirty-three years he held this position, and that exclusively on the Epistles. Otherwise, he treated the Old Testament. He never once taught Lombard's *Sentences*, reflecting his conviction from Erfurt days that the Bible was far more valuable than the standard summaries of Scholastic theology. Luther participated in the usual formal disputations of university life, on a wide variety of subjects. Near the start of his teaching appointment at Wittenberg, probably in 1513–1514, he contracted with the city council to preach regularly at St. Mary's, the city's principal church, above and beyond his preaching assignments in the monastery. Thus, lecture hall and pulpit together provided the institutional forum where his dawning theological insights could reach the public.

At the meeting of the Augustinians' General Chapter in 1515, Luther was named provincial vicar, an important post for the politics of the order and the larger church. He had to oversee eleven Augustinian houses in Thuringia and Meissen and functioned as something of the order's number-two man for all of Germany behind Vicar-General Staupitz. The experience would serve him well in the various pastoral, disciplinary, and political assignments he would later have to handle in carrying out the reformation of the church.

Exegete of the Righteousness of God

Luther's theology developed above all through his practice of scriptural interpretation as a preacher and professor. For his early lectures Luther gave commentary, in sequence, on the Psalms (*Dictata super Psalterium*, 1513–1514), Romans (probably 1515–1516), Galatians (October 1516 to March 1517), Hebrews (1517–1518), and then the Psalms again (1518–1521,

Operationes in Psalmos). The Wittenberg professor clearly kept up with the best scholarship of the time. His lectures drew from the commentaries of the church fathers and the interpretations of the medieval exegetes but also depended on the humanists' new biblical and philological aids, like the textbook and lexicon of the Hebrew language by Reuchlin, the fivefold text of the Psalter with commentary by Faber Stapulensis (Lefèvre d'Étaples), the edition of the Greek New Testament of Erasmus, and *Annotationes* by Lorenzo Valla.

Luther's lectures, with all their theological richness, have been thoroughly—and polemically—mined by scholars in search of the exact time and content of a so-called "Reformation discovery" or "change" in Luther's thinking. This mining, which has not led to a clear consensus, has largely consisted of attempts to reconstruct from the lectures hints Luther gave about his development at a much later date. One key site of such retrospection is his preface to the first volume of the complete edition of his Latin writings, dated March 5, 1545.[14] The chronological details of these reflections are imprecise or ambiguous and need to be interpreted case by case according to the specific historical moment in which Luther uttered them.

Some of this retrospection reflects his personal experiences in coming to understand the concept of the righteousness of God (*iustitia Dei*) in Romans 1:17. At first, Luther said, he understood the term in the established sense of the philosophical tradition, that is, as *iustitia distributiva*, rewards and punishments justly assigned to us according to our actions. At the last judgment God will be righteous in pronouncing sentence in keeping with God's own nature. For the unrighteous, the sinner, God's righteousness can thus only lead to the punishment of eternal condemnation. For that reason Luther loathed the word.

But in reflecting closely on Romans 1:17, a new sense of

the term dawned on him. From the turn of phrase "the righteous shall live out of faith" (*iustus ex fide vivit*),[15] he came
to understand righteousness as a *gift* of God through which
God, through the power of faith, *makes* one righteous in an
operative and efficacious way and conveys the *gift* of eternal
life. In his reading of Augustine's *On the Spirit and the Letter*
(*De spiritu et litera*), Luther found confirmation of his new
understanding of related expressions in the Bible that spoke
of God's righteousness, God's strength, God's wisdom, etc.
Righteousness, through the efficacy of God shared in faith,
amounts to God making righteous the unrighteous human
being who, per se, is a sinner.

We must seriously doubt that Luther had one precisely dat-
able experience that left so strong an impression and bore such
central significance as to constitute his "Reformation discovery." Nevertheless, we cannot doubt that the insight that constitutes the core of Luther's so-called doctrine of justification
would broaden out into a fundamental theological critique of
the existing nature of the church and the prevailing Scholastic
theology. Certainly the radical consequences that flowed from
this insight only became clear to Luther himself in a gradual
process. The controversy over penance and indulgences functioned as the catalyst in this process; this conflict, in which
Luther was enmeshed from late 1517 on, moved his discovery
of the righteousness of faith to the center of God's relationship
with humanity. Importantly, Luther found this discovery, too,
authenticated in his reading of Augustine, the most important
father of the Western Church. As to a "Reformation discovery," then, between the insights provoked by the indulgences
controversy and Augustine's confirmation of it, justification by
faith became the "Reformation" teaching that radically called
into question the existing church and understanding of faith,
ultimately giving them a radically different form.

Given the peculiarities of their genre, Luther's lectures

provide only conditional information about his movement toward a "Reformation theology." They show a growing concern, first of all, for the literal sense of the Bible (*sensus literalis*); next, a monastic strain; and finally, an ever stronger orientation to ordinary Christian life that needed to be equipped to absorb the Pauline understanding of faith. Characteristically, in interpreting Scripture Luther took what the Bible says about Christ and applied it to his own implementation of faith, his own life. The lectures on the Epistle to the Romans show Luther's other principal inspiration, for the theology of grace that he discovered in Paul was confirmed above all in Augustine's polemic against Pelagius, a text that had only recently become better known and closely studied. Instead of trusting in his own strength of will over against God—which, according to Luther, was the characteristic mark of Scholastic theology—he followed the anti-Pelagian Augustine from the Romans lectures on. He defined a theological position of radical grace that excluded any possibility that the human will contributed to salvation.

This theology of grace did have some support, to be sure, in the tradition of the Augustinian Order, and it was not without parallel in contemporary theological discussion. But Luther's claim that it constituted the center of the biblical message gave it a definitive new quality. More strategic was his gradual winning over of the other theologians at Wittenberg to his understanding of Augustine. These included both Nicolaus von Amsdorf, one of his lifelong and most intimate friends, and Andreas Rudolf Bodenstein, called Karlstadt, who became his intra-Reformation opponent after their break in 1522.

Their "Augustine Renaissance" from 1516 on gradually became a kind of trademark for Wittenberg University, which at the time still had a low profile. Early in 1517 Wittenberg restructured its theological curriculum around the Bible and the church fathers, especially Augustine, radically devaluing

Scholastic theology and the Aristotelian philosophy at its base. The backing and support that Luther found among his colleagues in the first half of 1517 gave him a base for stepping out into the public in the second half of that year.

The first series of theses that Luther himself definitely sent to the press (*Contra scholasticam theologiam*) was based on a disputation that took place on September 4, 1517, and, as the title indicates, posed a fundamental attack on Scholastic theology.[16] At the same time, this was the first systematic theological text we know of that Luther took care to distribute himself. His theses were heartily welcomed. For example, the Nuremberg jurist Christoph Scheurl helped distribute them to the Universities of Ingolstadt, Cologne, and Heidelberg.[17] This nontheologian was convinced by, and even enthusiastic about, the Wittenberg theology's move to ground our relationship with God wholly on the saving grace of God while radically negating the role of natural human ability in that relationship.

In sum, if we look critically for some basis for a "reformation," we can conclude that Luther had laid one in the twelve years following his entry into the monastery. He had a key position within the University of Wittenberg and his Augustinian Order. As a university teacher and a monk, he was carrying out the official assignments entrusted to him, and was growing into them. He represented two of the most respected institutions of his day, a most significant prerequisite for his getting a hearing.

In 1517, Luder was ready to become Luther.

Prophet and Reformer

In late 1517 Luther gradually stepped into the arena of ecclesial, territorial, and imperial politics across Europe. His attack on indulgences unleashed a dynamic that would produce the most fundamental changes ever experienced in the Western Church. The effectiveness of this Wittenberg monk and professor of theology is beyond compare; it can only be explained on the basis of several factors structurally working together. None of them alone triggered the Reformation; only their interaction did.

First, many people were convinced by Luther's message and conduct. While the controversy about Luther's "heresy" ran on, sometimes little noticed by the public, he appeared in print as a generally nonpolemical, devotional author who knew how to communicate, in the ordinary language of the people, the basic elements of the Christian faith, like the meaning of repentance and baptism, the Lord's Supper and the Lord's Prayer, the Ten Commandments, Christian marriage, a Christian way to die, and the suffering of Christ. These flowed from his pen rich in meaning and aimed at the Christian's everyday conduct in the world. By the end of 1519, before the heresy proceedings against Luther had entered their final stage, twenty of his German titles had been disseminated in over 140 different editions. Besides these, there were the Latin texts in which Luther carried on his controversy with representatives of Scholastic theology and the Roman Church: twenty-five titles in over 110 printings through 1519. This powerful burst of publishing was unmatched in the previous history of printing.

Luther's success as an author in 1518–1519 showed with what acumen and what results this monk, who until then had hardly written a thing, could use the new medium of book printing to touch the nerve of his time. Luther proclaimed in print a Christian message focused on the basic document of the faith, the Bible, on Christ, on belief, and on the mastery of ordinary religious life, and he found an electrifying response. By the close of his heresy proceedings, the Wittenberg monk—still side by side with his colleague Karlstadt, who, after Luther, was the most influential publicist of the early Reformation—had won over numerous followers, above all from the cities. Some of them, particularly the most educated and—with their humanism—the most sensitive to questions of church reform and Bible interpretation, became important disseminators of Luther's thoughts and concerns, and then leaders in expanding the movement, sometimes quite independently. In short, the reasons that many were convinced by Luther are as complex as the forms by which they came to express their belief.

Luther's message also succeeded because of larger circumstances. Luther and the religious movement that issued from him could only gain a foothold and then sustain itself because the legal and political conditions of the Holy Roman Empire of the German Nation permitted it—indeed, favored and promoted it. The political system of the old empire was based on power sharing between the imperial center and the federated states. Any measures to suppress the Reformation remained the prerogative of city and territorial officials. This applied especially to the imperial ban imposed upon Luther and his followers by Emperor Charles V in the Edict of Worms (May 26, 1521). The decree placed Luther outside of the protections of the law, rendering him subject to killing by anyone, without consequence; it also forbade the distribution of "evangelical" writings.

Yet not a few local and regional rulers refused to follow the emperor's anti-Protestant politics, whether from religious motives, or from yearnings for greater political independence, or out of material hopes of seizing church properties, or out of a tangled mix of these, as was typical of the time. The emperor also faced acute military threats, especially from France and the Ottoman Empire, and these forced him again and again to make temporary political compromises with the party of heresy in his territories. With that the Edict of Worms was blocked or slowed down, and reform could go forward in sympathetic cities and territories.

Only in 1546, the year of Luther's death, did the emperor gain a free hand to try to wipe out Protestantism by force, but that failed too, ultimately because of the resistance of political leaders across the empire who saw in the prospect of domination by the emperor the worst danger to "German liberty." In the early 1520s the Reformation spread out and dug in, aided by the affinities between the communal ideas of Luther and his followers on the one hand and the legal, social, and political mentalities of the cities on the other hand. These affinities helped the Reformation become a political reality that then radiated from the cities into the territories.

Luther's message was also enhanced because he, as an insider, was able to subject the formal apparatus of the church to a merciless critique on the grounds of Scripture, Christ, and faith. As a consequence, it fell into a fundamental crisis of plausibility. On the face of things, this would seem most unlikely, because the church—at least in Germany—looked to be thriving. In the rich holdings of the devotional foundations; the flourishing confraternities; the fantastic operations of pilgrimages; the thriving indulgence campaigns; the boom in the building of churches, monastic complexes, and chapels—there were no storm warnings at all in the forecast for the church. The explosive strength of the outbreak that was the Reformation cannot be traced to any evident inner crisis in the late medieval church.

At the same time, in, with, and under all this colorful church piety ran a mood by turns critical and apathetic toward the Roman Curia. This mood was present in equal degree at all levels of society, both spiritual and secular. In the *Grievances of the German Nation* (*Gravamina nationis Germanicae*), the imperial estates regularly voiced their

protests against their financial exploitation by the pope and
the operations of church law, which—the complaint read—
led them around by the nose. Many of these accusations
were grounded in real evidence and aptly served Luther's
polemical arsenal; doubtless he and most of his German
contemporaries with him felt justified in making them. But
more important than the realities of the matter were the
sentiments behind the accusations. Rome seemed distant,
unspiritual, morally depraved; the Curia was a trading post
of benefice hawkers; the pope was very far from the epitome
of piety. From Rome you could expect betrayal; you nego-
tiated with it, you did not respect it. Nor did the inflated
promises presented by the great indulgence campaigns un-
leash waves of joy about the pope's sweet offer of salvation;
on the contrary, even before Luther stepped forward, they
fed skepticism as to their spiritual sincerity. As for the Curia
itself, it was headed by the Medici Pope Leo X, who viewed
Luther primarily as a political challenge, yet had no German
political strategy. Leo was fixated on threats of a Hapsburg
intervention in Italy, and hesitated to put the prince-bishops
and prince-abbots of the empire under any political obligation. All this contributed to feelings of resentment against
Rome, which Luther and his party knew how to exploit to
devastating effect.

And finally, Luther's message succeeded in part because
of precedent. The "discovery" that set in motion Luther's
"reformation" in the strict sense of the word—that is, the
process of restructuring the church—had precedents in various medieval strands of tradition, including those of the
Spiritual Franciscans, the Lollards, and the Hussite heretics. This pivotal insight came to Luther in 1520, when he fell
under the sentence of heresy. It consisted in the certainty
that the pope—not as a person, but as head of an institution—was the Antichrist. Luther's Antichristology, which

like everything he wrote spread like wildfire, constituted the moment in the early Reformation when a political idea became an apocalyptic movement.

From this point on many were convinced that history was relentlessly running to the end of its course; the last days were at hand. In that circumstance, what mattered was to purge all God-defying disorder in favor of an order conformed to God's will. The order of the day was to repent. The apocalyptic drive of the early Reformation movement, which was absolutely set afoot by Luther himself, and from which no one knew how to extricate himself better than he, essentially carried Luther's cause in its dynamic breakthrough until the catastrophic year of the Peasants' War (1524–1525). Even thereafter, for instance in connection with a threat from the Turks, apocalypticism remained a live current in the mental apparatus of the Reformation.

From these factors, then—Luther's persuasive abilities, the political structure of Germany, the estrangement of the empire from the papacy, and the apocalyptic wave of 1520—came the unique success of the monk and professor from Wittenberg.

Heretic

Indulgences were an additional provision for guilt relief that the church had first devised in the eleventh century and had since elaborated into a sophisticated system. They were designed to supplement the penance that all Christians were to fulfill upon their annual confession, by which believers could secure salvation instead of the damnation that was the due penalty of sin. Yet many sins would remain unconfessed at death, for whatever reason, and they still needed to be paid off; that happened in a long process of suffering and repentance in purgatory between one's death and one's eventual entrance into heaven. Indulgences served to shorten that "purging" process and could be obtained by an outlay of money. Better yet, purgatory could be completely avoided by obtaining a plenary indulgence, available only from the pope. By Luther's day these could even be bought on behalf of someone who had already died; the deceased's suffering in purgatory was promised to end immediately upon the purchase of an indulgence letter preissued by the pope. For a slightly higher price one could buy a so-called *Confessionale*, a letter of confession that served to absolve the purchaser in the face of death (*in mortis articulo*) at any point in the future (*semel in vita*); in other words, it guaranteed full release from the penalties of any sins that would accumulate from the time of purchase forward. This comprehensive spiritual insurance policy was tendered as a social tariff so even have-nots, who could not come up with money, could enjoy them. It was this set of indulgence practices that triggered the Reformation.

The plenary indulgence that outraged Luther had been issued to finance the construction of a new St. Peter's basilica in Rome, but the people who counted in regional politics brought different reasons than his to the issue. The St. Peter's indulgence was available for sale only in the church territories of Magdeburg and Mainz, for Albrecht von Brandenburg, the young archbishop of both, needed to repay the enormous debts he had incurred in getting a papal dispensation to head up two dioceses—a violation of church law. Albrecht would share fifty-fifty with the papacy in the proceeds of the indulgences sold in his territories. While Luther himself knew nothing about this background when he went on the attack, some of those who joined in his critique were far more interested in the financial side of the matter than he. Among them were Elector Frederick of Ernestine Saxony and Duke George of Albertine Saxony, both of whom forbade the sale of the new indulgence in their territories.[18] They resented the prospect of money flowing out of their lands to their Brandenburg archrival. In addition, Elector Frederick owned a valuable collection of relics at All Saints' Church at Wittenberg, which attracted pilgrims who could accumulate some moral credits by coming to venerate them. That is, Frederick resented the pope's unwelcome competition in the salvation market.

Luther, in contrast, was offended by indulgences because they violated his central understanding of Christian life as taught in the Gospel. Jesus's call to repentance,[19] wrote Luther in the first of his Ninety-Five Theses, did not involve the sacrament of penance as the church taught, but the whole life of the believer: "When our Lord and Master Jesus Christ said: 'Repent, etc.,' he willed the entire life of believers to be one of repentance" (*Dominus et magister noster Jesus Christus dicendo Penitentiam agite, etc.! omnem vitam fidelium penitentiam esse voluit*).[20] Further, the pope could only remit punishments for sin in this life, not beyond death, in purgatory. In any case, Luther taught, forgiveness for the guilt of sin belonged to God alone. Repentance through the power of faith freed the believer from the compulsion of having to escape the punishments of sin in this life by works or payments of pious compensation. Works that really please God—like prayer, charity, and fasting—flow spontaneously out of trust in God's forgiveness. Luther was expanding the basic monastic impulse, that all of life be one of repentance, to the life of all believers. At the same time, because forgiveness was a gift of faith, he detached the concept of repentance from the basic medieval idea that the essence of penitence lay in human merit, which thus staked a human claim upon God.

Luther's attack on indulgences struck at the core of the

church's received tradition, and the ensuing controversy was so intense because his questions impinged directly upon core church practices as well as church teaching. That is why his Ninety-Five Theses (*Disputatio pro declaratione virtutis indulgentiarum,* 1517)[21] were so earthshaking. Luther at first shared them only with some of his close colleagues at Wittenberg as well as, by attachment to a letter, Archbishop Albrecht, the ecclesiastical authority responsible for Wittenberg. He made them known to the wider academic community of Wittenberg on October 31, 1517, probably by hammering them onto the church doors, which functioned as the university bulletin board. At the beginning of 1518, he allowed them to appear in print with a comprehensive Latin explanation of the Theses, and a German writing that contained the central statements with his criticism of indulgences (*Sermon Concerning Indulgences and Grace*).[22] By the end of 1519 this short piece (it came to only seven printed pages) had come out in twenty-two editions. Publishing this sermon in the language of the common people was far more effective than the Latin theses, with their forbidding language. By then, however, a German edition of the Ninety-Five Theses had appeared at Nuremberg. Almost overnight Luther's name had become known to the educated and the literate.

Hostile responses came quickly. The first appeared at Frankfurt, from Johann Tetzel and his fellow Dominican Konrad Wimpina, who were in charge of the indulgence campaign. Others soon joined in. As the war of words proceeded, Luther's orthodoxy came under the scrutiny of church law. The process was initiated by Albrecht von Brandenburg, who officially asked the University of Mainz for an evaluation of Luther's writing, passing along a copy to the pope. Rome had to postpone any proceedings, however, until after the upcoming election of the Holy Roman emperor. The Curia wanted above all to prevent the election of Charles of Spain—and of the House of Hapsburg—and to that end was cultivating the support of Frederick, elector of Saxony and Luther's territorial prince.

The proceedings at Rome finally began in May and June of 1518; they ended with the promulgation of a papal bull threatening Luther with excommunication (*Exsurge Domine*) on June 15, 1520. During the two years in between, Luther, having in early 1518 solidified his political support in Electoral Saxony, unleashed a tireless publishing offensive. This involved making ever more clear and precise his position on the theological points in dispute. At the same time, the matter of indulgences and penance proved to have implications for three broader areas, and Luther did not hesitate to pursue these fearlessly.

First, Luther's blow-by-blow written exchange with the Curia theologian Sylvester Mazzolini da Prierio drew the question of the teaching authority of the church, especially that of the pope, into the center of the debate. Prierio, in a screed against Luther published in early 1518, adopted a crude papalism to argue that every teaching presented by the pope became an infallible criterion of the true faith.

Second, Luther's hearing before the Curia's legate, Cardinal Thomas Cajetan, at the Imperial Diet of Augsburg in 1518 relocated the theological axis of the controversy and pushed Luther to a new theological development. The meeting happened at the behest of Elector Frederick after Luther had been summoned to Rome; Frederick wanted to make it possible for Luther to issue a recantation, and on the safety of German soil. Cajetan pressed Luther with questions about his seventh thesis on indulgences.[23] Could Luther explain more precisely, Cajetan asked, how he thought believers may become certain of their personal salvation? For himself, Cajetan held that we can only be certain of the church's sacramental mediation of salvation, not of our own individual status. In reply, Luther argued that we can only be sure of salvation by availing ourselves of Christ's word of promise, based on justification by faith. It was now clear that not the penitential system itself but the relationship of Word and faith constituted the key theological issue at hand; this moved Luther to a fundamentally new understanding of the role of the sacraments and the role that the presence of God played in salvation.

Finally, things climaxed with the famous disputation held at the University of Leipzig from June 27 to July 15, 1519, prefaced by a considerable preliminary round of publishing. The argument pitted Johann Eck, professor of theology at Ingleslow, against the Wittenberg theologians, Luther and Karlstadt. In the course of the debate Luther came to argue from the Bible and history against the papacy's claim of power from divine right. Further, he denied the hierarchical placement of bishops over pastors and disavowed the infallible authority of church councils. The Bible alone was infallible, he insisted, and no church authority could promulgate doctrines or decisions that were not based on it.

Eck responded by citing the decrees of the Council of Constance (1414–1418) that condemned the theologians John Wycliffe and Jan Hus, hoping to trap Luther in their company.[24] But Luther welcomed the charge, and with that seemed to have been led into obvious heresy. From then on Eck worked in Rome with a fiery zeal to have Luther officially declared a heretic, and helped lead the curial commission that prepared the bull for his condemnation.

That bull, *Exsurge Domini*, listed forty-one of Luther's statements as heretical and ordered the destruction of the various writings that contained them. Luther was given sixty days to recant after receipt of the bull; the contract for its promulgation in the empire was given to Eck and Jerome

Aleander as papal nuncios. But the funeral pyres that were stacked up across the country to burn the "heretic's" writings functioned instead as advertising beacons that fostered solidarity with Luther and his cause. Meanwhile, Elector Frederick, pressed by the pope to compel Luther to recant, succeeded in getting the newly elected emperor Charles V to schedule a hearing for Luther at the next imperial diet, at Worms. This was a direct check against the binding force of papal decrees, postponing a sentence leveled by a theologically unambiguous finding of heresy per canon law. Frederick's appeal was a significant victory, gained by legal, political, and diplomatic means, for the strategic position of Luther's religious cause. The threatening but inconsistent process of establishing him as a heretic only increased public interest in him, which had already grown enormously in 1519–1520. Luther was now the charismatic leading figure of a movement that, from this point on, would prove impossible to quash. As a "heretic" protesting that he had been unjustly condemned without a hearing and boldly declaring that he was bound by Scripture alone, Luther emerged with an authority and power in the wars of public opinion that no theologian before him had ever possessed. With his command of print media both in scale and skill, he cast a spell over the public that turned him into a key figure in the politics of the empire.

The year 1520 was Luther's "wonder year." Anticipating papal condemnation, hoping that it still might not occur, and confident in the unshakable truth of his faith, Luther leapt up with a remarkable spiritual and literary creativity to reach the pinnacle of his career. In this one year he issued five seminal works that defined a whole new Christianity. In *The Babylonian Captivity of the Church*, coupled with his "Sermon on the New Testament," he caved in the foundations of the entire Roman Catholic sacramental system and built up a theology of evangelical baptism, repentance, and communion to re-place it, based on a system of Word, faith, and outward sign.[25] In the tract *On the Papacy in Rome*,[26] he sketched the basis for a German evangelical, as opposed to Roman Catholic, model of the church. In *Address to the Christian Nobility of the German Nation*, he reached a high rhetorical pitch in urging the emperor and princes to take up a rich, practical agenda for reforming the church in German style.[27] In perhaps his most famous tract of all, *The Freedom of the Christian*, he poured out faux pity on the bishop of Rome for being tied up in the strings of his Roman courtesans and lawyers, and appealed to all Christians to exercise the wonderful freedom Christ had wrought for them—by being of service to their neighbor.[28] Finally, in addressing his most controversial tenet in *On Good Works*, he showed how Christian ethics properly rested on the basis of justification by faith.[29]

The year climaxed on December 10, when his excommunication took effect. Luther responded with a gesture that in a certain sense followed from everything that had happened up to that point. But if the act was virtually inevitable, it still was very difficult for a son of the church who wanted to remain faithful; it felt like a burden that God had placed upon him. With trembling hand and shaky voice, he turned the judgment of heresy back upon the pope's church, accusing it of having fallen into irretrievable error. In front of the Elster Gate of Wittenberg, quoting Psalm 21:10 ("Because you have dragged down the truth of God, may the Lord drag you down today"), Luther committed to the flames copies of the canon law and some Scholastic books on penance and instructional manuals—and, as if by the way, the bull threatening his excommunication. Later he said this was the happiest deed of his life.[30] It was surely the most primal, audacious, and heartfelt, a monstrous provocation: the excommunication of the pope's church in the name of the certainty of the

Christian faith. Thus December 10, 1520, marks the "Copernican revolution" in the history of Western Christianity.

Two key scenes remained. In them Luther the writer became Luther the doer and thereby earned the halo of enduring charismatic leadership in the Reformation movement. First came the dangerous trip to the Diet of Worms; it turned into something of a triumphal procession. His refusal to recant before the emperor and princes immediately turned him into a hero and martyr, a heretic whom one could kill without penalty, and a "saint." From the immediate wave of publications that recounted the confrontation at Worms favorably to Luther and "the gospel," it was evident that he had turned the highest political stage of the empire into the most important platform for his cause. The second key scene was less spectacular but hardly less effective: it consisted in Luther's return from Wartburg castle where Elector Frederick had sequestered him for security purposes on Luther's way home from Worms.

Luther spent nine months at the Wartburg in isolation and suffering, but also in a concentrated bout of work that laid the foundations for a new church, faithful to the gospel. He drafted his German translation of the New Testament, the model for all ensuing Bible translations into the various European vernaculars, and the key spiritual and theological resource for carrying out the full transformation of the church. At the same time, in his treatise *On Monastic Vows* (*De votis monasticis*),[31] he tore down the walls of the monastic system, lowering it from its elevated status as a superior form of the Christian life. Rather, he put everyone who had been baptized on an equal plane, all standing with like immediacy before God. Beyond that, by publishing his postils (homiletical helps) on Advent and Christmas, he set out a model—which soon became a standard—for how gospel preaching ought to be done.[32] His return from the

Wartburg to Wittenberg in early March 1522 allowed him to turn all this work into practice. He seized back the initiative of the Reformation enterprise from the hands that had taken control of it during his absence—above all, Karlstadt's.

Even though Luther's move back home came against the counsel and will of the elector, the Wittenberg Reformation from this time on would proceed under the political protection of the territorial authorities. Also under *his* authority. The former monk, now bearded and wearing secular dress, returned to his pulpit and lecture hall to assert command of the Reformation. He partnered with the most respected co-workers but did not suffer competitors. This almost immediately precipitated a break with Karlstadt. The key issue revolved around the demand of Karlstadt and his "radicals" that any and all biblical commands be literally and immediately put into practice. Luther instead had regard for the existing order of things and for the "weak," those members of the community who were as yet undecided about the reform. This first schism of the Wittenberg Reformation presaged future divisions—evident in the full emergence of Anabaptism, in the rise of Thomas Müntzer and the peasants he attracted, and with the reformers of upper Germany and Switzerland with whom deep-seated differences in the interpretation of the Lord's Supper would have to be thrashed out.

Teacher

Naturally, Luther's life could not continue at so high a pitch. In one dramatic five-year stretch, 1517–1522, he had burst forth with a new understanding of the Christian faith that church law, power, and politics could not suppress. Now he had to follow through with the consequences. These included everything from the structure of the worship service, to theological and religious education, to the various relationships of church and social life.

Luther helped lead the makeover of the church in the cities and territories of Electoral Saxony, but also far beyond them. He concentrated on basic models of church organization and operations: the election of pastors, communal finance ("The Community Chest"), the Sunday liturgy, church visitations, and ordination. These quickly acquired normative status in church domains that were bound to the Wittenberg Reformation, whether within Germany or beyond. In the changes they wrought, Luther's models still exert influence today.

Luther's influence on Protestant religious culture was all-powerful and many-sided. He was a composer of hymns. He authored two catechisms (1528–1529): the *Small Catechism* for basic church instruction and the *Large Catechism* for preachers and evangelists. Above all, he was an ingenious translator of the Bible (his first "Complete Bible" appeared at Wittenberg in 1534). All these, too, are still felt today. Still, the spectacular years in which Luther's name was on everyone's lips and, to many, offered a symbol of hope for the whole nation, indeed for all Christianity, gave way to polemical but unspectacular years. More and more he settled into becoming a respected teacher of a particular church that, according to canon law, was an "impossible possibility."

For Luther's image, the mid-1520s marked a dividing line. His polemics against the rebellious peasants in 1525 were as unlucky in timing as they were sharp in rhetoric. They appeared after the rulers' armies had already carried out their gruesome massacres, and therefore seemed to give these a stamp of approval. Luther's break with some fellow Protestants on the question of the Lord's Supper also cost him many sympathizers. As the religious-political and theological fronts solidified, a clearer definition of the religious and institutional character of Reformation churches emerged. If these were legally unstable, they were nonetheless likely to survive. Thus, Luther's star now shone beside the stars of other Reformers. Theirs might not glow as brightly as his, but then again, his no longer radiated over the entire Christian world but only over its Protestant part. Wittenberg University, where Luther along with Melanchthon, his most important colleague, presided, commanded a powerful sphere of influence and would remain for years to come the most heavily attended institution of higher learning in the empire. For decades Wittenberg served as the educational platform and recruitment base for a Protestant intellectual elite in many European countries as well as the various German states.

As long as Luther lived, his word had greater weight than that of any other theologian. But it was no longer the word of a "hero of the people" or a "darling of the nation," just of an experienced and unbending church leader. His picture, which had been dispersed in massive quantities and countless variations by the Cranach school, now intimated a man of unshakable conviction and confessional loyalty. His marriage to the erstwhile nun Katharina von Bora (1499–1552) in June 1525 produced six children, two of whom Luther himself had to bury. This bound the former monk fast to the joys and sorrows of ordinary life, increasing his pastoral sensitivity, and offered a model of the Christian household that remained a prototype in German evangelical parsonages, and German culture, for centuries.

Thorns

For most of his life Luther enjoyed robust health. In the late 1520s, however, as he approached his forties, some troubling symptoms emerged: angina pectoris, a ringing in the ears; after 1536 kidney stones and headache. He interpreted his physical sufferings as had the apostle Paul,[33] as blows from the devil. The fact that he did not suffer martyrdom, as had other messengers of the gospel, sometimes caused him anxiety or even despair, for it went without saying that suffering for the sake of the truth came naturally to his biblically formed worldview. Often he sensed that he was close to death, and gratefully availed himself of the pastoral comforts of his friend and faculty colleague Johannes Bugenhagen, Wittenberg's city pastor and a highly influential reformer of the church in northern Germany and Scandinavia.

Luther died in Eisleben, the town in which he was born, on February 18, 1546. By the standards of the day, at age sixty-two he was old and full of years. He had traveled to Eisleben to reconcile conflicts between the local counts. The details of Luther's "blessed death" were precisely recorded by his friends and entourage, and were published far and wide.

His public persona, however, commanded the enmity of the pope's church even to his grave. Shortly before his death Luther had heard of a publication in Rome, *On the Lies of Doctor Martin Luther's Death*,[34] which reported, among other things, that Luther's corpse, in compliance with his will, had been placed on an altar where it was to be "worshipped like a god."[35] Over against that kind of blasphemy, Melanchthon's eulogy at the grave of his beloved and difficult colleague gave an apt measure of this human being, one that accorded with Luther's own self-concept. He was, Melanchthon said, first of all and above all "a servant of the Gospel awakened by God." That was not a bad start for remembering the most powerfully effective figure of the sixteenth century. Luther understood himself to be the chosen instrument of God's Reformation and was so remembered—in his own lifetime, and again and again afterward.

CHAPTER THREE

A Theological Life

God's Word and Luther's Teaching

Luther was not the least bit interested in constructing a theological system for the ages. Rather, his theology arose from reflection on the practice of faith under the Word of God amid the immediate circumstances of the day. It is always necessary, therefore, to keep the historical context of his writing in mind when interpreting his work.

Luther thought this especially true of his early writings when, as he looked back on them from 1545, he had zealously defended the cause of the pope out of fear of the last judgment.[1] Those pieces contained so many subservient concessions to the pope, he now thought, that they amounted to wicked blasphemy, an abomination. So the contradictions that his opponents spied in him might be ascribed to his early inexperience or to his ever-shifting contexts.[2] Likewise, when from 1537 on he was regularly urged to issue a monumental edition of his complete works, he was very hesitant to do so. Church history had ample warnings of the danger hidden in such a project, he said: "ever since they began to collect many books and great libraries in addition to and next to the Holy Scriptures . . . precious time for studying the scriptures [has been] lost . . . until the Bible lies forgotten in the dust under the bench."[3]

Finally, at the insistence of Elector John Frederick of Saxony, Luther set to work on what would be called the Complete Wittenberg Edition; it came out in nineteen volumes, twelve in German, seven in Latin, between 1539 and 1559. He seemed to have been persuaded by the need for accurate historical documentation: "If I did not permit their publication in my lifetime, men wholly ignorant of the causes and the course of events would publish them after my death, and so out of one confusion many would arise."[4]

Luther's assent to this complete edition had momentous consequences. From then on a great Luther edition has appeared every century: the Jener edition of 1555–1558, the Altenburger edition of 1661–1664, the Leipzig edition of 1729–1740 closely followed by the Walch edition of 1740–1753, the Erlangen edition of 1826–1886, and finally the Weimar edition, which has been ongoing since 1883. These established the most important framework for the reception of his work. The Reformer's expectation that his books "would not last long once the passion of our day has abated" was not fulfilled.[5] The monumental complete edition, which immortalized Luther in the annals of publishing, has loomed over those occupied with him ever since. It has required them to be alert to his historical circumstances, and has motivated ongoing reconstructions of his context and never-ending searches for the precious genuine pamphlets, the cheap prints of the day, which first made Luther famous.

Paradoxically, this accumulation of all his works, which Luther himself had a part in, made it more difficult or even impossible for Lutherans to comply with his own attitudes toward them: "I make the friendly request of anyone who wishes to have my books at this time, not to let them on any account hinder him from studying the Scriptures themselves. Let them put them aside as I do the decretals and excretals[6] of the pope [i.e., the statutes of canon law] and the

books of the sophists [i.e., the Scholastic theologians]. . . .
If I occasionally want to see what they did, or ponder the
historical facts of the time, I consult them. But I do not study
in them or act in accord with what they deemed good. I do
not treat the books of the fathers and the councils much
differently."[7]

On the one hand, Luther relativized the significance of
his writings in the face of Scripture and of theological works
that he highly praised, such as the *Loci communes* of Philip
Melanchthon, the Reformation's first dogmatics.[8] On the
other hand, when he insisted that his work was at least as
good as some writings of the fathers, he helped give it lasting
sway. A few titles he elevated above the rest: his catechisms
of 1529[9] and his theological polemic against Erasmus over
free will (*De servo arbitrio*).[10] If he deemed his other works
to be only of historical interest (*propter historiam*),[11] for these
he wished widespread distribution and lasting recognition.

These ambivalent judgments and wavering expectations
about his own literary legacy offer another parallel to his
dialectical judgments about himself and to the theology of
Saint Paul, in which the "foolish word of the cross"[12] became the criterion for the truth in the world. From Psalm
119 Luther gleaned three "rules" for a theologian's labors:
oratio, *meditatio*, and *tentatio*; prayer, meditative steeping
in the Scripture, and *Anfechtungen*, or attacks of doubt.[13]
The first rule proceeded from a clear logic: "First you should
know that Holy Scripture constitutes a book which turns
the wisdom of all other books into foolishness, because not
one teaches about eternal life except this one alone."[14] To
understand the Scriptures, "you should straightaway despair
of your reason and understanding" and beg the Holy Spirit
for assistance through fervent prayer.[15] The second rule, of
unrelenting meditation, Luther had already exercised in the
monastery: "Next you should meditate, that is, not only in

your heart, but also externally, by actually repeating oral speech and comparing it with the literal words of the book, reading and rereading them with diligent attention and reflection."[16] Only thus could one become a good "theologian," only by making new endeavors in meditating on Scripture, never being finished, never being satisfied with one or two readings. For God did not give his Spirit "without the external word."[17] Getting to know God is only possible by relentlessly rehearsing Scripture, like "chewing the cud." God finally becomes open to us by the strength of the Spirit descending in the word of the Bible.

Luther's third rule for the correct study of theology led on from prayer and meditation in and beyond the word of the Bible to the ambiguities of human experience. For no sooner does the Word of God come into the world through the Christian's appropriation of it than it calls forth the manifold contradictions of the devil. But one can become "a real theologian"[18] no other way. The assaults of doubt are the "touchstone which teaches you not only to know and understand but also to experience how right, how true, how sweet, how lovely, how mighty, how comforting is the Word of God."[19] Through the existential testing of the Word in episodes of doubt and temptation, amid harsh earthshaking experiences, faith first becomes authentic. Luther attested to the strength, and value, of these assaults in his own biography: "I myself (if you will permit me, mere mouse turd that I am, to be mingled with pepper)[20] am deeply indebted to my papists that through the devil's raging they have beaten, oppressed, and distressed me so much. That is to say, they have made a fairly good theologian of me, which I would not have become otherwise."[21] Such experiences in the interpretation of Scripture, carried out in combat with the church of his time, built the background of Luther's systematic understanding of theology. So he presented it, especially in the preface of the first volume of his German writings (1539), as a memorial for posterity.[22]

If theology for Luther is essentially interpretation of the Word of God, and if the Word of God is a dynamic, active reality in which, through which, and with which God acts in history, then faith must strive toward experience,[23] and only through experience[24] becomes knowledge as well as certainty.[25] The assignment to understand Scripture, therefore, can never be finished and surpasses every other mandate. In the last piece of writing we have from his hand, Luther claimed that he had "brought the Holy Scripture and God's Word into the light of day as had not been done in a thousand years."[26] He went on to formulate the most sober, perplexing, and quintessential wisdom that he had gleaned from his theological life: "No one can understand Virgil's *Bucolica* and *Georgica* [his poems about country and pastoral life] unless he has spent five years as a shepherd or a farmer. No one understands Cicero's letters, in my opinion, unless he has spent twenty years in the affairs of state. No one should believe he has sufficiently savored Holy Scripture unless he has led a congregation with the prophets for a hundred years."[27] It is experience alone that makes a theologian (*Sola autem experientia facit theologum*).[28]

Luther's concept of theology as human self-interpretation under the canopy of the Word of God accounts for the vital and at the same time fragmentary character of his work. Resolutely practical and oriented to experience, the interpretation of Scripture was always supposed to become concrete in the here and now. To break it off or not always take it up again would be to block the path of the speaking God, the path upon which God had come to us in the past and will always come back afresh in the future—in the Word.

This was theology in a new key, oriented against the Scholastic tradition on the one hand and the "Enthusiast" or radical Protestant approach on the other. The first type tried to pin down ultimate eternal truth in time through the certified tradition of the papal church. The second resorted to speculation released from Scripture—and surpassing it in authority—along with the individual experience of God. Over against these Luther insisted that only the all-excelling speech of God, always freshly understood and appropriated in Scripture, quickens life-saving truth for faith in the here and now. In his radical commitment to seeing God's will in Scripture and only in Scripture, Luther stood against the imposing mainstream of Western Christianity and the "progressive" spirits of his day. Luther carried on a conversation with his time only in conversation with God's speaking in Scripture in a clear, unmistakable, and unambiguous voice.

Luther's Bible

For Luther the Bible became the book of life. His inner relation to it originated in the depths of his biography and not from contemporary practices of piety, and eventuated in the firm foundation of the Reformation. Luther did not see a complete Bible for the first time until he was twenty years old, in the university library at Erfurt. He immediately began to read it, and with great relish.[29] Before entering the cloister he relied on a postil containing the Gospel texts for the church year.[30] In his bouts of despair in the monastery,[31] as he later recounted, he asked for a Bible and he received a Vulgate bound in red leather.[32] He read it, read it again, and then yet again (*incepi legere, relegere et iterum legere*).[33] Luther's mentor, Johann von Staupitz, was impressed by Luther's comprehensive and extraordinarily precise knowledge of the Bible.[34] The young friar found himself agreeing with his Erfurt professor Jodocus Trutfetter, that the Bible rated far above church tradition.[35] This was in opposition to another teacher, Bartholomew Arnoldi von Usingen, who adjudicated between biblical and ecclesiastical authority by repeating that only the church fathers made the Bible speak with one voice.[36] In this light Luther's placement of the Bible at the center of his spiritual interests was quite one-sided and not at all self-evident from contemporary theological practice.

From the start Luther read the Bible expecting to find in it answers to life's questions. That focus generated his life's calling, but also new insights, new questions, and new clarifications that deepened and expanded with new readings. Luther knew himself to be endlessly superior in Bible knowledge to all his contemporary critics, whether to the "right" or to the "left," from the pope's church or from his own ranks. For several years he read through the whole Bible twice a year, cover to cover.[37] He characterized his reading with phrases like "rapping on it" or "knocking on it" for it to open; he "stormed" it or "tasted" individual verses. Luther lived with and in the Bible; it provoked in him fears of death and provided him with experiences of salvation; it pulled him into God's history with humanity and became the mirror and rule for his life. His insistence, in controversies with Rome and with fellow Protestants, that he could only be corrected by the witness of Scripture stemmed from his conviction that he was captive to the Word of God[38]— and, at the same time, that he was right on the one central truth of Holy Scripture. By the standards of previous church history, his was a striking one-sidedness toward the Bible, and it stemmed from his certainty that the Bible did not speak with many voices or so obscurely as to need church interpretation, but with *one* central message, the gospel of God's love in Christ.

Luther's viewing of the gospel—the "Sermon of Christ"[39]

and also "what drives us to Christ"[40]—as the pivot of the biblical tradition was hermeneutically radical at the time and also guided his epoch-making work of translation. He pointedly approached the Scriptures as "a good message, good tidings, good news, a good report, which one sings and tells with gladness."[41] Luther overturned the traditional hierarchy within the biblical canon dating back to Jerome and still followed by Luther's Wittenberg colleague Karlstadt. In this approach the Law took priority over the Prophets, the Gospels over the Epistles, and within the Gospels, Matthew over John. For Luther, by contrast, the value and significance of any biblical text were determined exclusively by whether, and to what degree, it not only treated the story of Christ and his works but also cast him as the mediator of God's salvation: "So too, it is not yet knowledge of the gospel when you know these doctrines and commandments, but only when the voice comes that says, 'Christ is your own, with his life, teaching, works, death, resurrection, and all that he is, has, does, and can do.'"[42] This one gospel is God's good news, which Christ "gives to all who believe, as their possession, everything that he had; that is, his life, with which he swallowed up death; his righteousness, by which he blotted out sin; and his salvation, with which he overcame eternal damnation."[43]

For Luther the good news first becomes perceptible at the very beginning of the Old Testament in Genesis 3:15 and runs like a thread through the Law and the Prophets. In the Psalms, he says, the living voice of Christ can be heard. The weightiest theological motive for his bitter tirades against the Jews, but also against Christian Hebraists, which piled up especially in his older years, was probably grounded in their negation of Luther's biblical hermeneutic, which regarded the Old Testament as essentially a witness to Christ. From his concentration on the "Sermon of Christ," a hierarchy emerged for Luther in the New Testament: the Gospel of John, the Epistle to the Romans, and the First Epistle of Peter constitute "the true kernel and marrow of all the books,"[44] for they present how faith in Christ overcomes sin, death, and hell, and yields the gifts of life, righteousness, and salvation. It was by this criterion of "gospel-icity" that Luther measured the rest of the New Testament. The Epistle of James, for example, he judged to have "nothing of the nature of the gospel about it";[45] likewise, the Epistle to the Hebrews, the Epistle of Jude, and the Revelation of John were placed at the very margin of the Lutheran canon, relegated to the back of the New Testament without their own numbering. For the Old Testament, the complete Luther Bible, which first appeared in 1534, followed the ordering of the Vulgate, although it placed the Apocrypha—books that are not included in the canon but nevertheless are recognized writings—in an appendix. While Erasmus and Karlstadt regarded the essential criterion for canonicity to be a book's validation by church tradition, for Luther it was the objective, theological-hermeneutical criterion of "whether it drove us to Christ." With this singular perspective the Luther Bible has a distinctive theological coherence that, along with its masterful language, probably accounts for its epoch-making and persistent significance.

Yet certain challenges face us in understanding Luther's Bible translation. For one, it did not stand at the start of his reformation path; he was not even the first one in the Wittenberg circle to publicly demand a Bible in the vernacular. That honor belongs to Karlstadt, who pushed that agenda already in 1519, consciously joining Erasmus of Rotterdam, the humanist church reformer, who advocated Bible reading by the laity as had no other. Erasmus's pioneering edition of the Greek New Testament in 1516 made responsible exegesis of the original text an unavoidable necessity; and from the early summer of 1521, translations of single books of the Bible had started to appear, based on the Greek text or on Erasmus's new translation of the Latin. The majority of these partial, pre-Luther translations of the New Testament probably breathed the spirit of Wittenberg, and the leading classes in the cities made the cause of a vernacular Bible into an ever-widening movement.

When Luther placed himself at the head of this movement, he gave it a new direction. For him, the goal of the German Bible was not, as with Karlstadt, to give the laity more spiritual independence so as to mobilize them for church reform. Nor was it primarily, as with Erasmus, to make the clergy feel competitive pressure from the laity so as to spur them toward further education and interest in reform. Luther wanted to promote the Word of God itself and make faith in the gospel possible. He wanted to accomplish this through a complete edition of the New Testament. And with the help of his introductions to the New Testament as a whole, and to its individual books, with which he supplied his edition, he hoped to give the laity the ability to tell the difference between the shell and the kernel, the law and the gospel, Christ and the world.

The hermeneutic Luther laid out in his prefaces contradicted the position on Scripture maintained by Karlstadt, his faculty colleague. For Karlstadt the Epistle of James, simply because it was included in the church canon, held equal weight with Paul, even though the first teaches a righteousness of works and the second the righteousness of faith. Here appeared the first tear in the early Wittenberg theology. Among the many who agreed with Luther's first principle of "Scripture alone" (*sola Scriptura*) were not a few who understood it differently; Karlstadt was the first.

Luther's plan to translate the New Testament, in order to provide support and comfort for the "true church" in its struggle against the Roman anti-Christians, seems to have originated during a short visit to Wittenberg, coming from the Wartburg, in early December 1521. Melanchthon pressed him to this task first of all because the partial German translations in circulation threatened to tear the New Testament apart; even worse, they relegated the epistles of Paul, Luther's most important texts, to the background.[46] At the same time, Melanchthon was worried about the upstart "Wittenberg movement" that had appeared that summer. This was something new: laypeople declaiming prophecies independently of any explicit word in Scripture. At the end of December the so-called Zwickau Prophets showed up, led by the cloth-maker Nikolaus Storch and onetime Wittenberg student Markus Thomae Stübner. They claimed to have received a special revelation, argued against infant baptism—the first such argument in the Reformation—and generally disparaged formal worship services and church offices in the name of immediate prophecies in the Spirit. Did not the book of Joel foretell just these sorts of manifestations for the end times, when the Spirit would be poured out?[47] In the Zwickau Prophets elements of the pre-Reformation Hussite and Waldensian "heresies" were appearing in Reformation circles, affecting their former pastor—and erstwhile Lutheran—Thomas Müntzer as well as Karlstadt. Luther's Bible translation, in making the explicit word of Scripture (*verbum externum*) available for the full understanding of the literate laity, would be a strategic countermeasure against this Radical Reformation spiritualism no less than against the principle of tradition in the pope's hierarchical church.

Within just eleven weeks at the Wartburg, Luther drafted his New Testament translation on the basis of the original Greek texts and the Vulgate. After a thorough philological revision by Melanchthon, who had excellent Greek, in September 1522 the so-called September Testament made its debut. With that the proscribed "heretic" established the most important foundation for the further spread of the Reformation and the emergence of the Protestant church. Luther's example was widely influential outside of Germany, stimulating the translation of the Bible into various national languages. Wherever the Reformation became successful, a vernacular translation of the Bible followed—sometimes constituting the very first literary document of that nation. With Luther's translation of the New Testament the Reformation became definitively a Bible movement.

While the September Testament was still being prepared for printing, to which Cranach added a series of woodcuts on the Revelation of John, Luther began to work full steam on his translation of the Old Testament from the original Hebrew. For the next twelve years he kept at it, along with some of his closest co-workers, especially Melanchthon and the Hebrew teacher Matthias Aurogallus, until the complete Luther Bible appeared in print. Whereas with the New Testament Luther had been concerned above all with presenting the unity of the books, for the Old Testament he had to take pragmatic considerations into account. He first published a series of manageable partial editions: in 1523 the first five books of Moses, and in 1524 the historical books (Joshua through Esther), the poetic books (Job, Proverbs, Ecclesiastes, and the Song of Solomon), and the Psalms.

Then the enterprise stagnated. Luther fell ill and the university had to relocate to Jena because of the plague (September 1527), during which time more and more demands piled up on him. Translating the Prophets proved to be extremely difficult linguistically. To top it off, in early 1527 there appeared the first complete German translation of the Prophets by the humanist-educated Anabaptist leaders Ludwig Hätzer and Hans Denck (the so-called Prophets of Worms), so Luther's Old Testament work devolved into a competition. Despite criticizing several of its details and the use that Hätzer and Denk had made of Jewish assistance,[48] the Wittenberg reformer had to make due acknowledgment of their work. In light of their considerable publishing success, it was clear that Luther would have to issue a comparable edition in parts. When his *Prophets All in German* finally appeared in 1532, he considered this work, though it had turned "truly sour,"[49] to be his best translation of all. The German text alone, he claimed, furthered understanding as much as reading many commentaries together.[50] For the Apocrypha, those writings not included in the Hebrew canon and which, according to Luther, "are not to be considered equal to Holy Scripture and yet useful and good to read,"[51] he drew more on the help of his colleagues Melanchthon and Justus Jonas.

Finally, in September 1534 the complete Luther Bible could appear, adorned with the elector's seal of approval, prefaces by Luther, and 117 woodcuts from the Cranach workshop, mostly finished at his direction. The first edition of three thousand copies seems to have quickly sold out. Slightly amended reprints appeared in 1535, 1536, and 1539. Between 1539 and 1541, with the help of a commission of experts, Luther overhauled the whole translation.[52] Final responsibility for what could be very complicated translation decisions rested with Luther himself, who frequently "had [to] search and ask about . . . a single word for two or three or four weeks."[53] Even after this Luther continued to work on improvements without ceasing until his death; he viewed his Bible translation as probably the most important achievement of his life.[54]

The enormous success of the Luther Bible proved him right, for between 1522 and 1546 it sold half a million copies in some 430 partial or complete editions. The Luther Bible was a significant milestone in the history of language and in the development of German in particular. Although German was in the process of standardization, also in written form, before Luther, this was accelerated by the printing production of Wittenberg, which for the most part avoided dialect. As a monument of the German language and a source of linguistic inspiration for religious and profane literature alike, the Luther Bible lived well beyond church bounds into the twenty-first century. Catholics translated the Bible into German as well, sometimes in complete dependence upon the Luther Bible, but always in contradiction and competition with it, proving in their own way that the need for a lay Bible was not to be suppressed, regardless of the attempts of the Council of Trent to do so. The turn to the vernacular Bible, which Luther's translation effected in such a richly influential way, transformed Western Christianity as a whole.

Luther had undertaken his translation "as a service to the dear Christians and to the honor of the One who sitteth above us."[55] Yet he was aware of the epoch-making linguistic import of his work. With some justice he reproached his traditional critics, who were completely immersed in the language world of Latin, that they had first learned to "speak and write German"[56] from his translation. He faulted the "Prophets of Worms" for "trail[ing] very far behind his German."[57] Whereas the pre-Reformation translations of the Bible into German typically imitated Latinate styles, Luther wanted to honor the particularities of the target language and transmit them accordingly: "We do not have to inquire of Latin letters how we are to speak German. . . . Rather we must inquire about this of the mother in the home, the children on the street, the common man in the marketplace. We must be guided by their language, the way they speak, and do our translating accordingly. That way they will understand it and recognize that we are speaking German to them."[58] Whenever the translation might fail to capture the sense of the original Greek or Hebrew, however, Luther demanded a close dependence on the original. For the problem of translating particular "dark" places in Scripture, comparable "clear" places had to be brought in, for Scripture was its own best interpreter (*scriptura . . . sui ipsius interpres*).[59] Finally, it is Christ who gives clarity to Scripture; it needs to be read coming from him and going to him.[60]

Luther's attempt to relate his German translation to the language world of ordinary people did not mean that the Luther Bible was folksy or renounced an artistic, rhetorically rich structure. On the contrary, his sentence constructions made for ringing, rhythmic figures of speech. There were choice alliterations, like *"Stecken und Stab"* for "rod and staff" in Psalm 23, or *"zittern und Zagen"* for the "fear and trepidation" of Mark 14:33. Luther used rhymes like *"Rat und Tat"* for "word and deed" in Proverbs 8:14; "singing and ringing" in Sirach 39:29. He also made up words like *Feuereifer* (fiery zeal), *Denkzettel* (memo note), *Herzenslust* (desire of the heart), and *Morgenland* ("morning land," i.e., the East). These bear witness to Luther's creative ability with language. The success of his Bible validated his boast over against the "papists": "I can translate, they cannot."[61] More than any Bible translation before or after him, Luther's Bible was his personal work.

Lecture Hall and Pulpit

History placed upon Luther the historical burden of becoming the head of a heretical church. He did not seek this role. He meant to be a blameless monk, a scrupulous priest, the teacher who, in conscientiously fulfilling his office, "knocked" on the door of Holy Scripture with his life's questions. The church he loved had robbed him of all this with an uncompromising severity. With an academic's trust in the strength of an argument, in following the Bible with its binding authority as *the* primary document of Christianity, and with his growing theological insights, he had attempted to lead a fruitful reform of the church and its theology. After all, as an obedient son of his church he had suffered from its loss of credibility and its rote practices of piety, from the loss of genuine repentance that stemmed from the system of indulgences promoted by a church hierarchy given over to worldly pomp.

Unlike other contemporary voices critical of the church, however, Luther spoke from deep down within the heart of Christianity, from the center of its holiest source, "from the very voice of God." That in any case was Luther's conviction. Without it, he could not have accepted the heretical role that he was obliged to take on by a church that had become guilty before God and God's prophets.

Given the state of the church, Luther's claim was all too apt; given reality, he was exceptionally naïve in thinking that simple theological truth could, and must, put the church in order. Thus he lost himself between the roles of obedient son and condemned heretic. Yet without this righteous naïveté he would not have been able to assume the burdensome task of building a new church. He accepted it by carrying out a reversal of rhetorical roles, and in high dudgeon. Mounting as it were the platform of an evangelical papacy, he pronounced the Roman Church and its law to be heretical in a thundering adaptation of pontifical speech: "I, Martin Luther, called a doctor of Holy Scripture, an Augustinian of Wittenberg, notify all men that by my will, advice, and help, the books of the pope of Rome and some of his disciples were burned on the Monday after Saint Nicholas Day in the year MDXX [i.e., December 10, 1520]."[62] There was now no turning back; Luther had become the oracle of the "true church," and in that name pronounced sentence upon the pope.

The institutional supports that served Luther in the exercise of this unheard-of role lay near at hand: his university post as professor of theology and his preaching office in the city church of Wittenberg. The legitimacy of both callings was indisputable: the first, from the territorial lord and his monastic order; the second, from the Wittenberg city council.[63] The fact that, as a mendicant, he hardly earned anything from them should have benefited his reputation even more. His independence from the clerical benefice system gave him a moral advantage over his critics that he knew how to exploit. Only his preaching contract brought him a modest personal income, of about eight gulden; for a long time that was all he received. Nor did he earn anything from his lectures or by the publication of his writings. Only when Luther entered into marriage in 1525 did he obtain a regular personal income adequate to his circumstances.

The significance of these offices for Luther's activities can hardly be overestimated. The specific possibilities and challenges of the two decisively shaped the work of the Reformation. As a preacher who had been stepping into the pulpit in Wittenberg weekly, sometimes daily, from 1513 on, Luther became a well-known and highly esteemed personality in local affairs. Ironically, the popularity that the preaching doctor from the Augustinian cloister gained in the city and university laid the foundation for his later Reformation work; he retained the support of Wittenberg for the rest of his life. Long before the conflict over indulgences, Luther had established confident relationships with the Wittenberg city councilors and their electoral counterparts, with citizens and students, relationships that must have been grounded in and nourished by his regular preaching. When the movement for reform took a direction he did not like during his enforced absence at the Wartburg, he succeeded immediately upon his return in turning things quickly and thoroughly to the course he had in mind. That would hardly have been possible without the Wittenbergers' confidence in him and high expectations of him.

For Luther as a preacher, it was both possible and necessary to unfold the theological insights of his exegetical work in a comprehensive and understandable way before the good people of the city. The monk who moved, taught, and comforted the people of Wittenberg had always kept the practical dimensions of his piety in full view. Spiritual and ethical practice was thus of the essence in Luther's theology, not some secondary, external aspect. The two sites of his calling, pulpit and lectern, made this close association possible. The seemingly effortless ease with which Luther could get to the heart of things in the songs he composed and in his popular *Small Catechism* for children and common folk reflected the many years his theology had been steeping in the weekly rounds of Wittenberg. Some of his early publications developed from sermon series—for example, his interpretation of the Ten Commandments,[64] which quickly became successful. Many of his texts went from his desk to the printing press via the pulpit. This was especially true of his great early successes by which he became known as a "religious author of the people."[65] Among the talents that allowed Luther to become a reformer, therefore, central place has to be given to Luther's second vocational activity, as a city preacher.

His enormously popular printed sermons were accompanied, after 1522, by unauthorized related texts of at least partially dubious authenticity. They were printed outside of Wittenberg and pumped into the market. In some cases Luther felt it necessary to issue revised or corrected versions, pointing out that he submitted all his writings to Wittenberg

University's censor[66] and allowed them to appear exclusively at Wittenberg. Besides, they bore the elector's seal of approval and trademarks like the Christ Lamb and the Luther Rose that, from 1524 on, he used in printing the Bible. By such methods the Wittenberg professor tried to protect his own words in a world without copyright.

Luther carried on the double burden of his two vocations until his death. In doing so he remained visible and present to his community and a living testimony to the students, rulers, and famous scholars who made the pilgrimage to Wittenberg. Some of the later university theologians and church leaders of Lutheranism who studied there in the 1530s and 1540s found that he made a greater impression on them in the pulpit than in the lecture hall. During the roughly three and a half decades in which Luther was professor, his lectures were exclusively exegetical—not the prescribed course but one reflecting his self-understanding and definition of theology's proper task. From early on he used the commentaries of the church fathers and some of the work of medieval exegetes along with the learned humanist resources of the day. In his last lectures, on Genesis, beginning in 1535 and continuing for the rest of his life, he consulted rabbinical commentaries more closely, if for the most part critically. A great number of his lectures gave birth to commentaries that went to press either from Luther himself or on the basis of student notes. In the 1520s he chose to lecture on the Old Testament writings that he was busy translating. With the leading humanists, he gave pride of place to the literal or historical sense (*sensus literalis seu historicus*) as opposed to the allegorical (*sensus allegoricus*), although he did not relinquish—in fact, could make excessive use of—the latter when it seemed to make theological sense.

Luther's commentaries always appropriated the biblical text within present circumstances. Some of them became key texts for the intellectual socialization of his contemporary readers and subsequent generations of Lutheran theologians: for example, the so-called *Small Galatians Commentary* (delivered 1516–1517, published in 1519), the *Large Galatians Commentary* (1531, published in 1535), his second lectures on Psalms (*Operationes in Psalmos*, 1519–1521), and the *Genesis Lectures*. With the discovery of his manuscripts since the beginning of the twentieth century, the early lectures have moved to the center of interest in Luther research: the first lectures on the Psalms (*Dictata Super Psalterium*, 1513–1514), on Romans (1515–1516), and on Hebrews (1517–1518). On the other hand, at the time, they had influence only on those who heard them, and thus allow little inference regarding their reception history. In any case, the continuity of his pastoral and academic activities kept Luther at some stages of his career from becoming completely burnt out by the polemics of the day; even more, they established the groundwork for his ongoing Bible translation.

The University of Wittenberg was a special place. As Luther said, it was situated "at the edge of civilization,"[67] far from contemporary centers of power, business, and culture. The city itself numbered some 2,000 to 2,500 inhabitants and was, next to Torgau, the residence for the Ernestine branch of the Wettin nobility. Significantly for the history of Luther and the German Reformation, the university there had only been founded in 1502, so when Luther joined the faculty, he faced no towering authorities and obligatory traditions. The ruling territorial lord, Elector Frederick, was pursuing ambitious goals in founding his new university. From the start it stood in a particularly competitive relationship both with the old Saxon (now Albertine) territorial university of Leipzig (founded in 1409) and with the city university of Erfurt (founded in 1392) in the Electorate of Mainz. Elector Frederick's protection for Luther in the indulgences controversy not only made the Wittenberg professor famous but also served the political aims of the university. The size of its student body first increased somewhat—in 1517, 242 students; in 1518, 273—then soared upward by leaps and bounds: in 1519, 458; in 1520, 579. Wittenberg soon outstripped all the other universities in the empire in enrollment and remained at the top for the rest of Luther's life, except for the usual intermittent vacillations. While the rest of the German universities were driven into fundamental and sometimes protracted existential crises by the Reformation, traditionless *Leucorea,* to use the Greek name for Wittenberg, captured the future Protestant elite in church and society to a degree unparalleled in the previous history of German higher education.

Naturally, the reason for this did not rest with Luther alone. From the 1520s on, it was often the case that students came to Wittenberg because of Luther but remained because of Melanchthon. As a teacher, organizer, and educational reformer in the liberal arts and theology, Melanchthon, who had been called to be the professor of Greek at Wittenberg as a twenty-one-year-old scholar in 1518, executed the redesign of the Reformation's academic program. Luther's main contribution to that probably lay in recognizing his talent and in collaborating with him on curricular reform. Otherwise, he let Melanchthon's creative "didactic imagination" unfold freely. The establishment of Greek and Hebrew language study at Wittenberg, the first German university where it succeeded at all, made this institution in a small Saxon city into the most modern university in the empire, and sealed the close relationship between "humanism" and the "Reformation" far beyond the conflict between Luther and Erasmus. Wittenberg's leading role in the contemporary university world proved to be essential for the breakthrough and implementation of the "new teaching" inside and out-side of Electoral Saxony.

The unique role it played in the Reformation made Wittenberg the intellectual center of Lutheran Protestantism, a place it held well into the seventeenth century. The young university also gained favor because it had a predominantly young faculty. The instructors' sense of having something to prove in light of their own and their institution's youth, coupled with the expectation of students who had chosen a university without a name, created a productive tension, furthered collegial exchange, and initiated a new kind of relationship between professor and student. When Luther and Karlstadt traveled to Leipzig in the summer of 1519 for the disputation with the high-profile Johann Eck, they were accompanied not only by the rector of the university and some faculty colleagues but also by a shock troop of some two hundred Wittenberg students. The controversy over Luther involved the corporate identity of the university as a whole, and its students came to their professors' aid by sometimes dubious means. Although Luther distanced himself from those, one nonetheless has to credit the students with a central role in pushing the dynamic of the early Reformation forward. Their mobility helped spread the new ideas, and their enthusiasm in stepping up as preachers and agitators in other places helped multiply them. In Wittenberg itself, especially during Luther's stay at the Wartburg, they supported the process of radicalization, demanding that church reforms be implemented. Sometimes this "Wittenberg movement" had the markings of a student revolt, a youth movement precipitated by intellectuals; it seems to have been the first case of the kind known to history. The professors were ahead of the students; teaching theology, the humanities, and social sciences, coming from within the church to initiate and carry out an uprising against the church, they were mostly in their early thirties.

As a friar and professor, Luther could count on a basic social recognition that essentially guaranteed him a hearing, at first chiefly among the educated. In this light it was crucial that the Reformation proceeded from a university and that its first advocates were professors. Luther was well aware of this himself. Especially for those in his own camp, his doctorate in theology legitimated his claims for authority, first against the "papists" and later against the "Enthusiasts." Luther had only ridicule and scorn for the self-reinvention of his Wittenberg colleague, the secular priest Karlstadt, who laid aside his academic titles, donned the gray frock and felt hat of a peasant, let himself be called "Brother Andrew," and took to describing himself as a "new layman" as befitted his new elevated esteem for the spiritual status of laity. Becoming pals with students or the lower strata contradicted Luther's conception—actually, deep conviction—of the God-ordained social inequality between people.

Luther's office as professor and his role as preacher preserved his authority over those he had to speak with, those he had to comfort, and those he had to teach. When this was threatened, he demanded that the other party stay in line. Such occurred during his visitation to East Thuringia in August 1524, which he undertook at the suggestion of Elector John Frederick. The region, in the orbit of Thomas Müntzer, had more recently come under the sway of Karlstadt, who had retreated to a pastorate in the city of Orlamünde in Saaletal after his conflict with Luther in 1523. Karlstadt promoted a program of congregational reformation that emphasized strong lay participation and included interpreting the Bible without the guidance of clergy; nor did he draw back from dramatic protests against the established church—for instance, smashing images and storming monasteries. For

Luther, eruptions of this sort were uncharitable acts against the "weak," those members of the congregation who were not yet firmly rooted in the evangelical faith.

He saw political insurrection in it besides. On his visit to Orlamünde Luther refused a city council delegation the customary honor of doffing his red-tasseled doctoral biretta.[68] In their letter the Orlamünders had addressed Luther as a "Brother in Christ," to which he retorted: "You did not grant me my [doctoral] title, even though some rulers and lords who are my enemies recognize it and don't deny it; therefore I have received your letter as a message from an enemy."[69] By asserting his formal authority and entitlement in situations like this, Luther hoped to overcome "disorder." In fact, this confrontation simply manifested the irreconcilable conflict between his methodically controlled academic interpretation of the Bible and the spontaneous lay reading that they claimed in the name of the freedom of faith. They were no longer willing to accept the limits placed upon them by a narrow-minded "biblical scribe" who represented the social and political establishment. Experiences of this kind hardened Professor Luther, but also illustrated that too much was expected of him.

The devastation of the Peasants' War and the experience he gathered in the official church visitations he conducted from the mid-1520s on strengthened Luther's conviction that a clear hierarchical order was founded alike in God's command and in political reason. His political conservatism, which Müntzer already criticized and which has been adumbrated by the Marxist school of Reformation research, certainly for this intellectual had nothing to do with an opportunistic accommodation of the high and mighty of the time. It grew far more out of his biblically rooted theology of order. God had established three estates for the maintenance of the world and for the upbuilding of the church: the teaching estate (*status ecclesiasticus*), the ruling estate (*status politicus*), and the producing estate (*status oeconomicus*). In this rather static model of society, each estate had its clearly assigned duties; at the same time, all of them together shared obligations to the church. Yet the concept also offered points of departure for salient critique. If a particular estate failed in its designated purposes or overrode its assigned limits—if, for example, representatives of the clergy promoted political agitation, or political authorities hindered the proclamation of the gospel—then it threatened to corrupt God's prescribed order and deserved a disciplinary intervention. Luther's conservatism, based in his theology of creation, was a "realistic" option amid the political conditions of his time. Furthermore, the head of the heretical church had civil authorities to thank not only for his personal survival but also for the success of his reformation work. If he noticed them at all, Luther had no use for the utopian social models that were circulating at the time. Given the imminence of judgment day, what was important was to preserve the legitimate order, not to create a new one.

In sum, Luther derived and developed his concept of the Reformation from a conscious awareness of the authority of his teaching office in the lecture hall and pulpit. In his model, political and ecclesiastical elites were expected to work closely together. The most important disseminator of the Reformation message was supposed to be pastoral instruction, above all from the pulpit. He reformed pulpit speech in his own idiom via his postils, which gave model interpretations of the texts assigned for Sunday sermons. His *Large Catechism* was supposed to secure the basic theological training of the pastor, but from the official church visitations that he made, especially in 1528–1529, he learned that much was in disarray and that a "useful literature" was needed to implement suitable praxis in the Reformation churches. Luther also remained a preacher and professor as acting visitation commissioner for the state. He had formulated "true doctrine" in such a way that, for the most part, only a few educated pastors of the first generation of Reformation clergy and their congregations could use and appropriate it. With the *Small Catechism* (1529) he laid it all out for the base, the children. In it Luther interpreted the Ten Commandments, the Lord's Prayer, and the creed, the most sacred basic texts of Christianity, for the world of his time; it became the "iron ration" for the life of Christian people. In zeroing in Christian teaching on *my* God, *my* faith, and *my* salvation, he brought together the learned and the lived faith, his own faith and that of evangelical Christianity.

God's Creation and the Civil Order of the World

As a condemned heretic, Luther lost the protections previously provided by his monastic order and church tradition. The Word of God, personal certainty of faith, and the legitimacy of his office destroyed his old world, while simultaneously opening possibilities for a new one. In this new world he was free within and "free as a bird" without— that is, in serious jeopardy of death. Outside the protective space of Electoral Saxony, he was liable to anyone's vigilante justice, which severely limited his mobility for the last quarter-century of his life. He also feared assassination in Wittenberg, because he had many enemies—and believed himself to have even more. Thus, by the contemporary standards of educated people, Luther lived in a narrow but not a closed world.

The discoveries made by the European voyages of exploration back in his childhood, which we today recognize as having world-historical significance, were of little interest to him. He barely noticed the very extensive travel literature and reports they generated. On the other hand, the economic effects that the huge Spanish and Portuguese gold imports from Latin America had on Europe were not hidden to him. His insistence on a just price and moderate rate of interest was tied to an economy of commodity exchange, and aimed at enforcing the standard of Christian love as an ethical value over against the boundless accumulation of capital by distant trading giants like the Fuggers of Augsburg. Thus, faraway worlds interested Luther chiefly to the extent that they affected his own, the community entrusted to his care.

This orientation is also reflected in the way Luther dealt with reports from alien worlds, like those about the Ottoman Empire or the Jews "in the neighborhood." The first was a world that might advance to threaten his own, the second was a world that was actually nearby. In such cases Luther was most concerned over the dangers posed by the foreign entity, and even helped distribute pertinent literature in this vein that had come to his attention—typically, warnings about the menacing approach of the Turks or the supposed malice of the Jews. Luther felt this obligation by virtue of his concept of office; he was certain he would have to give an account at the last judgment for the souls that had been entrusted to his care.

Luther's mental world was not extraordinarily wide or narrow. It was more intensely directed by the Bible than was true of any theologian before him. He could not muster any comprehension of Copernicus's astronomical theory, which provided the basis for what proved to be the revolutionary heliocentric worldview. He dismissed it as an intellectual's craving for admiration: "Whoever wants to be clever must agree with nothing that others esteem. He must do something of his own. That's what this fellow does who wishes to turn the whole of astronomy upside down."[70] Besides,

Joshua commanded the sun to stand still,[71] precluding the notion that it is the earth that moves. In this sort of judgment it becomes clear that Luther always considered the Bible right, and that warnings against vain and idle curiosity (*vana curiositas*), which were deeply rooted in him from the monastic tradition, had entered into his bone and marrow.

On the other hand, he was open to inventions and insights that promised immediate benefit for humanity, and could even praise them as gifts of God. Naturally, this applied above all to the printing press, but also to innovations in horticulture, fisheries, and agrarian and mining techniques. He remained skeptical about pharmacology and medicine insofar as they grew out of dietetics. He allowed dietary rules no influence over his life at all: "I eat what I like and will die when God wills it."[72] In the hierarchy of the three graduate faculties, medicine naturally ranked lowest for him because it involved only the human body, reason, and temporal life.

As for the faculty of law, which to his annoyance was not prepared to submit to that of theology, he felt deep reservations that seemed to grow over time. Certain factual questions Luther believed he could opt to clearly decide from the Bible, rejecting any other source of input. This was the case with the prohibited proximity of kinship in marriages. But the jurists, also the Protestant ones, deemed it necessary to stay with the prescriptions of canon law. The same applied to secret marriages, that is, engagements made without the parents' permission. These were recognized by canon law and some jurists, but Luther opposed them, appealing to the commandment that required children to obey their parents. His uneasiness with lawyers went beyond particular questions of church order or policy decisions in secular affairs, however; it was more fundamental. Their sober, calculated "worldly cleverness," their formalism, their inclination to concoct binding regulations contradicted his individual, personally oriented way of dealing with human concerns. For example, when a rich burgher from Augsburg sent him an expensive cup and the lawyer involved asked for a receipt, Luther found the request intolerably mistrustful: "I have written enough books to fill the world and you treat me as a *vir obscurus,* 'an obscure man.'"[73] In his table talk Luther vented his ire in stronger terms: "Before I would send him such a note, I would rather shit and piss in the cup."[74] Luther considered lawyers for the most part to be devious people who were only after their own advantage and wanted to either make others suffer or undermine human trust. His understanding of Christian living as a genuine, spontaneous orientation toward one's neighbor, growing out of faith, was for him fundamentally incompatible with the calling and spiritual disposition of the lawyer.

Because Luther's concept of the world was essentially stamped by the Bible, he had a special eye for concrete circumstances and perspectives. The beauty of nature particularly impressed him. In the last year of his life, reading a volume by the Roman natural philosopher Pliny, he noted: "The whole creation is the most beautiful book or Bible in which God has described and painted himself."[75] In sermons, lectures, and letters he always found nature useful as a parable. He elucidated the wonder of Christ's bodily presence in Holy Communion by invoking the strength of light; the spring thaw served as a parable for the working of the Holy Spirit; tasty freshwater fish or the agility of his dog Tölpel became a reason to ponder God's wisdom and goodness as Creator; the quarrels of the jackdaws and crows that he observed while quartered in Coburg castle during the Diet of Augsburg in 1530 seemed a fitting image for the proceedings going on there that he, as a hunted heretic, was forbidden to attend. Readings in the book of nature expanded and enriched his readings in the books of Scripture and history.

Luther's world was not "narrow" in the sense of his feeling personally constrained. On the contrary, the religious world, which with the help of the gospel this condemned and driven man arranged for himself, was *his* world. It suited him and enveloped him like a warm and welcome shelter, because it was a world precisely determined by God, a world filled by God's presence in the Word and in the bread and wine of the sacrament. In Luther's world, God was not out there somewhere but very nearby. God was not a distant transcendent reality only of interest for having set the bounds of time and space; such a distant and hidden God is nothing for us and none of our business.[76] The God of Luther was the one we "should avail [ourselves] of for every good and take refuge in amid every need,"[77] the God of trust and faith of the heart. Such a close God engenders trust, creates a shelter by his presence, and wards off the threatening, hostile world with his healing wings.

Luther's worldview was conservative, yet tied to an utterly revolutionary concept of a God who dynamites the set order dividing heaven, the world, and hell: "We say that God is no such extended, long, broad, thick, high, deep being, but a supernatural inscrutable being who exists at one and the same time completely in each and every seed, whole and entire, and yet in all and above all and outside all created things. . . . Nothing is so small but God is still smaller; nothing is so large but God is still larger; nothing is so short but God is still shorter; nothing so long but God is still longer; nothing so broad but God is still broader; nothing so narrow but God is still narrower and so on. He is an inexpressible being above and beyond all that can be described or imagined."[78] This religiously salvific, circumscribed cosmos, encompassed by God, is *creation*. Not creation only in the sense of a primordial act of calling into being that which was not, but more than that, creation in the sense of sustaining the world ever and anew. Luther's certainty of God went with him into the world and made it possible for him to have a positive view of the world after the monastic world had broken down—even after the ultimate head of Christianity, the Roman pope, was exposed as simply an enemy of Christ, the very Antichrist, and even when the political powers under the aegis of the emperor manifestly deserved more suspicion than trust. Through episodes of doubt and near despair, Luther's certainty was confirmed again and again: God was lord of the world and of history. Despite all persecutions and every assault of the devil, he knew, from the wellsprings of faith and the record of his life, that he had been saved from all his enemies and was comforted for Christ's sake.

After leaving the monastery, Luther lived irrevocably "in the world," that is, in the sphere of ordinary vocations and social responsibilities. His departure from the cloister had gotten much attention, of course. In his pioneering work *On Monastic Vows* (*De votis monasticis*),[79] written while he was still at the Wartburg, Luther leveled the Reformation's characteristic attack on monasticism. In stigmatizing the legal, compulsory character of lifelong vows, he had set off a flood of exits from convents and monasteries. In the name of evangelical freedom, which was a godly right and a godly gift, he had broken the binding power that bent conscience under formal dictates, and more clearly established that every Christian was obliged only to the promises made before God in baptism. This passion for evangelical freedom theologically demoted the monastic or priestly aristocracy and in its place warranted a religious equality that gave everyone the same rights and obligations of Christian freedom before God. Yet Luther wanted to let the monastic way of life continue on a voluntary basis. To him this was nothing but a preservation of freedom; his critics naturally reproached him for inconsistency. His personal life exhibited the same paradox in that this authoritative liberator of monks and nuns continued to appear in public, down to October 1524, in the garb of his order, living on—with no apparent changes—in the Augustinian monastery of Wittenberg. For all the convulsions that Luther unleashed in world history, his Wittenberg address and the elementary bounds of his everyday life never changed from 1512 to 1546. Since he no longer understood himself to be a monk, however, he no longer lived in the religiously segmented world of the cloister but in regular civil society.

Some dramatic episodes of Luther's life were marked by the head-on collision between his understanding of society and vocation and those of other worldviews. A severe case of this sort took place in the Peasants' War, the widespread military-political explosion of 1524–1525 that today is counted as a revolutionary uprising of the common people. The crisis came to Luther's attention relatively late; his perspective was based largely on personal observations from the Thuringian-Saxon area of the uprising. He hardly had— perhaps could not have had—a clear idea of the full scale of the upheaval, which shook wide parts of the empire. That in itself was fateful, however, for just because he was Luther, whatever he said had public impact across the entire empire, whether he meant his remarks for a specific situation or not.

In Luther's life and in the history of the German Reformation as a whole, the Peasants' War marks a deep dividing line. First, with it the number of pamphlets published in the language of the people dropped significantly, and thus the contribution that lay writers would make to contemporary debates. At the same time, the relationship between religion and military force ominously moved to the fore and remained there.

Through the Peasants' War Luther lost the support of broad sections of the common people, those who had identified their demands for social justice in accordance with the divine law with the Wittenbergers' struggle for the freedom of the gospel. Nothing so badly damaged Luther's reputation among the revolting peasants and their city sympathizers as his publications during this episode. This was especially tragic because he was one of the few intellectuals of the time who had a thoroughly positive relationship with the peasant estate. Luther was completely estranged from, say, the arrogance spread by humanists against the "dumb," clumsy, brutish peasant. Reformation publishing elevated the worth of the peasants by its stock figure of the *Karsthans*, a shrewd, self-educated, rhetorically high-flying Christian farmer toting a two-pronged fork; this would have been unthinkable without Luther. Much of the tragedy of his fading popularity must be attributed to Luther's seeing peasant motivations far too much in light of Thomas Müntzer's apocalyptic announcement that the kingdom of God was at hand, which led his troops to inscribe slogans on their banners promising to annihilate unbelievers by force of arms. Luther's almost obsessive fixation on this main enemy from his own camp distorted his view, for Müntzer's theology had hardly penetrated the peasant ranks the way that Luther insinuated. If Müntzer became a central figure of the uprising from 1523 to 1525, it was mostly Luther's doing.

Under the pressure of these events the tone and tendency of Luther's writing changed dramatically. His first pamphlet on the matter (*Admonition to Peace on the Twelve Articles of the Peasants in Swabia*)[80] still clearly and explicitly recognized the social distress of the peasant estate and the coresponsibility of the princes, lords, and spiritual prelates for their grievances; in subsequent tracts this would slip away completely. Naturally, the change was triggered first of all by Luther's sense that the peasants were perverting the Reformation message for their own social and political demands. Then too, having his cause identified with that of the peasants risked losing the backing of the civil authorities who to this point had made the success of the Reformation possible. Finally, Luther was probably outraged by the first impressions made by the peasants revolting in Thuringia, and had come to the conclusion that, whatever their earlier complaints, they had radicalized beyond measure. To suppress their chaotic revolt, therefore, seemed to him the authorities' foremost Christian duty.

We do not know in detail what Luther actually saw and experienced during his travels through the region of the revolt. He might well have been dependent on one-sided information and interpretations from the counts in his native territory of Mansfeld, who carried out the military counterattack against the peasants. In any case, it is clear that he was shocked by not being able to get through to the peasants with his sermons. In Nordhausen, for example, as he pointed to the crucified Christ and admonished patience, he was mocked and drowned out by the clanging of the church bells.[81] To the rebels whom he had tried to reach in his travels through Thuringia, he became a representative of a hated regime. He could not get through to them with the Word, the only lawful means at his command, and that embittered him. Therefore, the devil had to be at work. Luther's pamphlet *Against the Robbing and Murdering Bands of Peasants*[82] could hardly have been composed before the beginning of May 1525; in any event, it probably appeared in print very shortly before the decisive battle of the Peasants' War at Frankenhausen, on May 15. The tract implied full license for the brutal murder of the peasants. Luther's traditionalist opponents found it easy to paint him as the prime author of the uprising and therefore, ironically, as the one chiefly responsible for the thousand-fold slaughter that the raging coalition of rulers mercilessly carried out.

In this episode Luther, the brilliant publishing strategist, had been overrun by events. If his call to suppress the uprising might still seem justified, certainly his call to kill the peasants as a meritorious religious act would have to count as contempt for human beings. In his postmortem on the event, *An Open Letter on the Hard Book against the Peasants*,[83] his sharp criticism of the victors for their immoderate acts hardly equaled his enraged tirade against the peasants whom Müntzer had incited to revolt. Very few of his contemporaries noticed that he scolded the princely murderers of Frankenhausen as "rabid, raging, mindless tyrants,"[84] "beasts,"[85] and pigs, and reproached them for humiliating Müntzer's pregnant wife. In allowing himself to take the role of a political agitator without any strategic calculation, Luther had gotten swamped; he was in over his head.

Luther's publications on the Peasants' War marked the low point of his ethical and theological work. But to conclude that the Reformer, stuck in his world as a theology professor, was politically inept does not do him justice. To the contrary, the success of the Reformation that he initiated was due in no small measure to his ability to gain the trust of and then persuade civil rulers in city and country alike. Luther's most successful pamphlet of all, *Address to the Christian Nobility of the German Nation*,[86] from the summer of 1520, along with other topical texts of the early 1520s (such as *On Temporal Authority*, 1523, and *Whether Soldiers, Too, Can Be Saved*, 1526),[87] brought fundamental clarity to the relationship between the gospel and politics, "church" and "state." Luther combined this with a critique of the pope's church that rang true to many of his contemporaries by endorsing most of the *Grievances of the German Nation (Gravamina nationis Germanicae)* against Rome, which had been under advisement since the late fifteenth century and had been passed as official resolutions in the German imperial diets. The papacy, so Luther informed the various ranks of rulers in the empire, did not observe its assigned spiritual duties but instead had usurped the right of Christians to interpret the Bible and had placed itself above civil authorities. As the sorry condition of the church had been recognized since the High Middle Ages, Luther's unsparing diagnosis could invoke well-established stereotypes and, with that, win the agreement of the politically responsible.

His diagnosis, like his prescription, took as a core assumption that the church was responsible for the salvation of souls, and the state for outward order. "Disorder," then, arose when either the state arrogated authority over religion or the church pursued worldly political interests. In this "two kingdoms" doctrine, God rules both church and state, but each has its own "instruments" that always have to be differentiated: for the state, the sword and the law; for the church, the gospel. Yet in emergencies, such as the present deformation of the church that had come about under the papacy, the laity in general, and especially those in political office and bearing sovereign authority, had the mandate—indeed, the duty—to carry out the reformation of the church. In a proposal he put forth in 1520 (to no avail), Luther suggested convening a German national council that would mandate church reform for the whole empire. Still, a fundamental differentiation between "church" and "state," religion and society, faith and politics characterized the realism of Luther's political theory. This was rooted in the pioneering work of Western intellectual history, Augustine's *City of God*, and insisted that differentiating eternal salvation from earthly well-being was necessary to both correctly understand and properly guard the interests of both.

In this light, we must say that, caught as he was in the throes of the Peasants' War and of his fixation on Müntzer, Luther was not willing to harvest the full analytic potential of his political-theoretical insights. Critics from his own camp saw the Spirit of God withdraw from him.[88] He knew that Müntzer's death "was his responsibility."[89] He had killed Müntzer with his pen because Müntzer, he was convinced, wanted to kill his Christ.

Christian Fellowship in the World

The solitary life did not agree with Luther's faith or personality. Throughout his life he searched for human fellowship and lived in community: in the home of his parents, at school, at university, as a monk, and later as a father who, together with his wife, Katharina née von Bora, took charge of the "whole house" gathered in the former Augustinian convent. To this house belonged, besides the children, the domestic servants; close and distant relatives of the family, either from his or his wife's side; ten to twenty students as paying guests, some with tutors in tow; and visitors—altogether, some thirty-five to fifty people, barely fewer than the monastery. The household, often supplemented by friends and colleagues from the city, gathered together at meal times, at festivals, for home devotions, and on other occasions.

Luther freed up certain times of the day for prayer, a custom that carried over from his time in the monastery. These were free in form, though not without strong directives, as he set out in *A Simple Way to Pray for a Good Friend*.[90] During meals they sang, and afterward Luther would sometimes interpret a psalm. Thus the Augustinian monastery turned into an evangelical "house church," an exemplary place of Christian piety. In his *Small Catechism* Luther laid out a foundation for an evangelical piety[91] that would combine the sincerity of being Christian with a resolute life in the world. The model was certainly tested and implemented in his own household. The efficacy of the *Small Catechism* for Lutheran piety, which has lasted well into the twentieth century, we can attribute to its real-life rootedness in Luther's own house church.

A visitor to the Luther house in the early 1540s mocked the strange assortment of people living there—young girls, students, widows, and old women—and ventured that many people would feel sorry for Luther amid all this commotion. But the ideal ambience of an educated man, per contemporary conventions of habit, decorum, and "self-fashioning," was not one that Luther sought. By the standards of the day, his was certainly an eccentric living situation—a former monk living in a former monastery. Yet this living space, the habitat of the community that surrounded the heretic condemned to hell, was to Luther "heaven on earth." Somehow he must have liked the everyday hubbub in which people were born and died, laughed and prayed, cried, cooked, brewed, had deep thoughtful discussions, and played. He never complained about it and certainly had the power to change things if he had wanted. Though the possibility of a solitary lifestyle was certainly on offer to him from 1521 on, it seems he never gave it serious consideration. He searched out and relied on human fellowship.

His isolation in the Wartburg when he was under the elector's custody was probably the most literarily productive period of his life, yet it was a time of personal suffering. He missed the exchange with his intimates, with friends, colleagues, students, his "congregation"; he suffered from loneliness and seems to have shown symptoms of psychosomatic illness, which he interpreted to be an affliction of either God or the devil—in any case, as a personal "suffering of the cross."[92] His dangerous decision to return to Wittenberg was prompted by the "untoward movement introduced by our friends in Wittenberg to the great detriment of the Gospel."[93] His responsibility for the gospel, which—as with Paul[94]—Luther claimed to have received "not from men but from heaven alone through our Lord Jesus Christ,"[95] became concrete in his responsibility for the congregation of those who believed in the gospel. This responsibility included the obligation to protect the gospel from false teaching.

The gospel for Luther was to be publicly proclaimed, resounding everywhere to engender trust in the atonement of God in Christ. Thus it gave birth to the congregation, the church of Jesus Christ. Accordingly, Luther's relationship with fellow Christians was dear to him. Luther forthrightly rejected mysticism as a road to salvation because it assumed an unacceptable concept of self-justification—that people by means of spiritual introspection could build up a relationship with God from their side and come closer to God, step by step, on their own initiative. Even more, Luther opposed mysticism for its privatistic and solipsistic traits. Precisely Luther—the apostle of the personal certainty of faith, the pastoral theologian who insisted that the turning point of one's relationship with God, one's very surety of salvation, lay in the "my" of each person's faith—emphasized the role of fellowship in the Christian life perhaps more than any theologian before him. The gospel itself engenders fellowship and needs fellowship; it has to be spoken out loud. The leading motif in Luther's ecclesiology is his understanding of the gospel as the Word of God that creates community and opens up relationships.

Luther's decision against the religiously segmented world of the monastery and priesthood was a decision for the real life of burghers, peasants, and noble lords—for the worldliness of the world. Although he framed this decision theologically as his personal discovery of faith in God's promise, in a practical and visible way it was only fulfilled during the

Peasants' War. This was not the result of some long-term strategic plan; it was the stroke of luck by which, on June 13, 1525, he came to marry the young erstwhile nun Katharina von Bora. For Luther himself, and for his movement in consequence, this was a decision carried out "for the world." To critics like Erasmus, but also to intimate friends like Melanchthon, the step seemed frivolous or at least unwise; he seemed to be choosing at this moment of earthshaking turmoil and collapsing foundations, with the world being turned on its head, to seek his own private happiness—or, as his traditionalist critics mocked in their uptight celibate pride, to let his lust come alive. Luther himself knew that the timing was hardly auspicious. At this low point of his popularity, to add suspicions of sexual impulsiveness to his burden could seriously injure this pious man, this learned leader awaiting martyrdom, this fearless preacher who dwelt in an aura of personal holiness.

Naturally, Luther felt a yearning to couple up; he was not made of stone. Besides, he made it no secret that the monastic project of killing off his earthly desires had failed.[96] Likewise, his father's wish for descendants had stayed with him. But despite having so successfully proven the Christian legitimacy of marriage, he had always deflected its possibility for himself, pointing to his prospects for martyrdom. Only under the enormous combined pressures of the summer of 1525—in the face of the Peasants' War debacle, in the conflict with Erasmus that wasted his strength and was costing him more followers, in the obvious ruptures that had occurred in his own camp, in the emergence of Anabaptism, in the conflict over communion with Zwingli, now joined by the Basel reformer Oecolampadius and his supporters in Strasbourg, Bucer and Capito—only then did Luther become inwardly free to bind himself completely to the world. Or, punning on the name of his wife, Katie (= *Kette* = *catena* = "chain"), only then did he allow himself to be tied to a "chain," to be "catenated" to Katie.[97]

A few weeks after the wedding, talking with his friend and erstwhile fellow Augustinian Wenzelaus Linck, who had married a year earlier, Luther mused with a touch of gloom: "I am bound to Katie and captured, and I lie upon my Bora and *scilicet mortuus mundo* [have died to the world]."[98] That is, precisely by allowing himself to step well and truly into marriage and the papacy's demonized sexuality, Luther erased the dividing line between the lay and religious spheres and so—paradoxically and ironically—achieved the highest goal of his monastic yearning, namely, to renounce and "die to the world."

Luther's untimely marriage with a woman whom at first he did not love, for whom he "did not burn" sexually, whom he nevertheless immediately liked,[99] should perhaps be taken as a kind of prophetic action-sign. Just as the prophet Hosea married a prostitute in order to represent, and make present, the sign of God's rejection of Israel,[100] so Luther married a holy nun to symbolize his freedom in God's order of grace and to point out God's judgment on the lying, hypocritical world of the pope's church. Some months after the fact, in talking to a man who had been impugned for entering a marriage that was illegitimate under canon law, Luther explained his own marriage thus: "I too have taken a nun in marriage, although I could have avoided it, and I had no other reason for it than to spite the devil, and his disciples, the bigwigs, rulers, and bishops, who in a simply irrational way wanted spiritual persons to be unattached. And I would gladly cause even more offenses if I only knew of more that would please God and annoy them, because in this way I cool down my temper as they rage and storm against the Gospel; for I do not give up, and the less they like it, the more furiously I'll push it."[101]

Thus, against the devil stepping forward in the guise of a moral apostle to spread the light of a false holiness and to propagate the lie that human beings could become justified before God by means of their ethical exertions and moral perfection, there stepped up an *enfant terrible* from Wittenberg with the prophetic spite of the gospel, turning the wisdom of the world into foolishness. Luther's decision for the world aimed at making the world more worldly, thereby robbing "righteous" people of the false glow of their presumed holiness. It was the revolt of a consecrated priest and former monk against the church whose dominion was based upon a derogation of life in the world in the name of the higher worth of the "spiritual" over the secular estate and vocations.

Luther's Reformation discovery of the worldliness of the world, his conversion from monk to citizen, rested on his radically egalitarian understanding of being a Christian: before God all Christians in themselves are sinners and by themselves are incapable of pleasing God. At the same time, however, before God all Christians are justified by faith. Before God all Christians are priests, and in their baptism are elected by the grace of God to be holy people. Through the gospel all Christians are freed and enabled, in fellowship, to become Christ for others. This radically egalitarian teaching about "the common priesthood" grew from the center of Luther's doctrine of justification, and with it he swept away the difference between clergy and laity as two estates, long thought to be qualitatively different in their relationship with God. With that a development of church history that had begun already in the second century came to an end. In Protestantism the "spiritual estate" no longer held higher value in the eyes of God, nor did the worldly vocations stand at a farther remove.

This revolutionary change in the Roman Catholic theology of office Luther first made popular in 1520, especially in his *Address to the Christian Nobility of the German Nation*. It set in motion a wave of lay protest that soon found Luther in well over his head. But unlike many who invoked his name and accused him of defecting from his earlier ideals, the Wittenberg reformer from the very beginning had upheld the necessity of church offices and laid out an ordered regulation for how they should be handed down. Ordained offices for the proclamation of the Word and the administration of the sacraments were necessary, he taught, by the very nature of the gospel as the promise of salvation, as the Word of grace. For this Word can never be said to oneself; it must be proclaimed to another. For that one needed the church, more precisely, the community of believers, who hear the Word, in whose circle the Word becomes efficacious, and who are brought back to faith through the Word time and again. In Luther's language the term "church" faded into the background in favor of other concepts that bore a less direct institutional connotation. Thus, he preferred to speak of *communio sanctorum*, the communion of the saints, or of the gathering, the multitude, the holy people. Above all, he used "congregation" or "community," or "Christianity" as the whole body of all Christians on earth, wherever found and however affiliated, even under the pope, under the Turks, everywhere.

Church for Luther meant the fellowship of those who hear the Word and believe. It is not bound to a specific legal-institutional entity; rather, it is entirely defined by elementary acts that first establish and then persistently renew it: the preaching of the gospel and the use of the sacraments instituted by Christ, baptism and Holy Communion. When it is instituted and upheld in that way, Luther said, a seven-year-old standing in its fellowship can know what the church is: "Namely, the holy believers and the little sheep who hear the voice of their shepherd. For children pray . . . [as the creed states], 'I believe in [one] holy Christian church.'"[102]

By dint of the priesthood of all believers, every member in principle may exercise the functions of proclaiming the Word and administering the sacraments, but not everyone is equally capable of doing that. To avoid confusion and unhelpful spiritual competition, it makes sense to invest this right in a particular person "by the command and consent of the others";[103] that is, this right is transferred by an act of delegation. Should such office-bearers leave their post for any reason, they step back into the status of normal members, fellow citizens and fellow Christians with everyone else. Because the fellowship of believers depends on the proclamation of the Word and administration of the sacraments, it is a visible, empirical entity in the world. But because faith in the gospel constitutes the nature of this fellowship, it is at the same time not of this world; it is hidden,[104] eluding visible perception, and is known only to God. Thus the church is the place where the gospel is proclaimed and heard in faith, but not all who hear the gospel believe.

This differentiation between the visible gathering and the community of salvation known only to God defined the specific ecclesial nature of the Lutheran heretical church. For God gathers true believers by Word and sacrament even in, with, and under the churchdoms that by the standard of evangelical teaching had to be condemned as corrupt—for instance, the pope's church. The boundaries of the visible church are not identical with the boundaries of the communion of the saved. Unharmed by the papacy's excommunication and unhindered by his own rejection of its legal basis, the duly proscribed heretic did not lock the theological doors but, in casting the church as a communion of believers, opened the way of salvation for Catholic Christians. As the communion of those who believe the gospel, the church is and always remains the church, the gathering of justified sinners; the church is and always remains the "world" and is "holy" only in that it knows itself to be accepted by God. An institution organized for salvation the way the church used to be, the church Luther declared to be heretical, is one that in the mind of the Reformer evangelical Christianity can never be.

After the 1520s Luther kept very busy instituting a new form of church organization in the cities and territories that joined the Reformation. He typically shared these responsibilities with his Wittenberg colleagues, especially Philip Melanchthon and Johannes Bugenhagen, the Wittenberg city pastor and superintendent who was Luther's father-confessor and his closest spiritual intimate. The abolition of Rome's canon law and legal structure in Protestant territories left an immense need for regulation. In these circumstances the Wittenberg city church and the professors of the theological faculty became the authority that vetted ordinands and supervised the Lutheran pastorate in the empire and abroad. This happened partly by default, but also because of Luther's charisma and the prestige of the university.

From his experiences as a church visitor, Luther gradually developed a lively sense of supracongregational church structures and connections—for example, the uniform transaction of ordination. He and his colleagues were regularly in demand as advisers on political matters and as spiritual counselors to individual pastors. Contrary to secular authorities, who tried to domesticate evangelical pastors and make them functionaries of the state, Luther gave them a stronger backbone. His structural conservatism regarding the church's external organization was ultimately aimed at finding socially acceptable solutions that served the fellowship and might win over to the gospel those members of the community who still adhered to the old ways. His organizational achievements, which in some part survived him, transposed his pioneering concept of the church into an institutional framework that, if a compromise, was set to endure historically.

The final results of Luther's church organization, of course, remained ambiguous because the impetus behind his radical understanding of the communion of believers could not be fully translated into institutional terms. He had one and the same aspiration for the house church, for Christian marriage, in gatherings and meetings of all kinds, everywhere that faith in the gospel was quickened and where love flowed out in response. In the preface to *The German Mass* (1526),[105] his vernacular liturgy that became something of a model, Luther connected freedom and order, "evangelical essence" and "institutional form," by the criteria of love for neighbor and the glory of God. Even though the use of Christian freedom is "up to everyone's conscience,"[106] it dare not be used for personal desires or profit but only as "a servant of love and of neighbor."[107] Thus, while "this external order [of the church] cannot affect the conscience before God,"[108] it is useful for the sake of our neighbor, for it establishes expectations, modes of relationship, and rules for regulating conflicts. By defining the public nature of the church as the private gathering of those "who want to be Christians in earnest," he relativized the institutional and emphasized the communal moment of fellowship as the right kind of order.[109]

Luther's religious poetry became an especially important source for teaching the evangelical faith to illiterate people. In what became a definitive mode of expression among his followers, he formulated what it means to be a Christian primarily in the first-person plural. One of his prayers is sung: "God the Father, with us stay / when we take our final breath / free us from our sin we pray / and help us have a blessed death."[110] Likewise, a communion hymn: "So let us feast this Easter day on Christ the bread of heaven; / the word of grace has purged away the old and evil leaven. / Christ alone our holy meal, the hungry soul will feed and heal; / faith lives upon no other."[111] The same holds for their anticipated victory: "Dear Christians one and all rejoice / with exultation springing; / and with united heart and voice / and holy rapture singing."[112] An anticipated victory: as with the individual Christian, so also with the communion of believers, the evangelical church in Luther's mind is defined not in being but in becoming.

Luther and His "Enemies," Actual and Imagined

The "enemies" of Christ were also the "enemies" of his prophet, Luther. In his children's song "Keep Us Steadfast" (1544/1545), he formulated unmistakably who were "the two arch enemies of Christ" that Christians, from early childhood on, were to break down by singing and bring down by praying: "Keep us steadfast, Lord, in your word, and stop the murder of the pope and Turk, who want to pull Jesus Christ your Son from your throne."[113] The two foes stood out for Luther against the looming end times. To emphasize his saturation in apocalyptic figures of speech—indeed, his thoroughgoing apocalyptic mentality—does not relativize his tendency toward valid instructions. On the contrary, for Luther apocalyptic and theological terms complemented and conditioned one another, having their common focal point in the papacy. For the papacy did not fit in the three estates of teaching, ruling, and producing that Luther saw established by God in creation for the rule and sustenance of the world. The pope's desire to dominate the emperor and so lethally confuse the *status politicus* and the *status ecclesi-*

asticus was sign enough of the imminence of the last days, when all order would be overturned. God's reformation, on the contrary, restores good order once again, just before the end. Whoever affirms that order has to despise and fight the papacy, which stands outside it. After 1529 "the Turk" would be added to the papacy as the apocalyptic enemy.

Luther's discovery that the pope was the Antichrist came in the context of his excommunication. The shock of being declared a heretic made it easier for him to reverse charges and carry out a full polemical offensive in retaliation. He employed every literary device at his command, at increasing levels of ferocity. He sustained his attack over the whole last quarter-century of his life, and near the end, sharpened it one more time in what turned out to be one of his last writings, *Against the Papacy in Rome Founded by the Devil*.[114] It appeared in 1545, within a year of his death. A psychologized interpretation of this enmity, emphasizing a tragic, obsessive fixation against the power that had consigned his person and work to eternal damnation, probably falls short of the mark.

For Luther the matter got its full significance from theological history. The papacy was that power that is at enmity with God and that, according to the relevant apocalyptic texts of the Bible, will at the end of time lift itself up over everything, including God and all that is in God's service. It will set itself up in the temple of God and pretend to be God; that is, it will be the Antichrist.[115] Since the Antichrist had now been discovered, there was no doubt that the last days were near. Certainly the "signs of the times" said so. The upsurge in the sciences and general culture, the victory run of the gospel like a "moving shower of rain," the printing press, the first martyrs of the Reformation, the persecuted little flock of true Christians, and many phenomena in nature, politics, and social life—everything testified that the end was at hand. Unlike the fear typically associated with a verdict in court, the last day for Luther and his followers did not raise apprehensions but raised the certainty that the true church would stand revealed; therefore, it would be a "dear last day."[116] The determination that the papacy was the Antichrist constituted Luther's lasting criterion of interpretation for theological history. For Luther the pope was an immovable enemy because he was the enemy of Christ. That theme was constant from its first appearance in 1520 on.

On the other hand, there was a certain process of development in Luther's position on the Turkish question. It was directly correlated with the Ottomans' surging military threat to Europe, evident in the Battle of Mohács (1526), where Suleiman I defeated the Hungarian army, and the subsequent Siege of Vienna (1529). In several close reflections prompted by these events—*On War against the Turk,*[117] *An Army Sermon against the Turks,*[118] *Preface to the Book of Daniel*[119]—Luther reiterated ideas he had stated earlier, but now with further clarification. He saw the Turks simultaneously as an enemy of Christ and a scourge that God visited upon Christians for unrighteousness that they themselves had not put aside.[120] Luther rejected the idea of a crusade against the Ottoman Empire—which his papal opponents unjustly interpreted as foreswearing defensive measures as well—and proposed fighting "the Turk" and his lord, the devil, with repentance and prayer instead. Any military offensive, he thought, should be regarded as an exclusively secular concern and not be stoked up religiously.

Luther studied the Qur'an from some medieval sources and a Latin translation, and even promoted its publication in Basel. For all that, he never doubted for a moment that Islam and its scripture amounted to a decidedly anti-Christian enterprise. The Qur'an dissolved faith in Christ by disputing the doctrine of his two natures, the divine and human, and by rejecting the doctrine of the Trinity.[121] Further, Islam disrupted civil order by its religious legitimation of robbery and murder; Turkish rule, therefore, constituted no "regular godly authority."[122] Beyond that, Islamic polygamy abetted immorality. Just as the pope was the Antichrist, so "the Turk" was the "very devil incarnate";[123] and just as with all enemies of Christ and with their father the devil, so "the Turk" knew how to transform himself into "an angel of light."[124] "The Turk" did so by fostering the impression of strong religious zeal—in turning away from other gods, in observing strict ascetic customs, and in his iron discipline, including the submission of women to men and people to ruler. Impressive as these were in themselves, according to Luther, so were the rejection of images[125] and the architectural achievements by which "the Turk" offered a beautiful, high-cultural advertisement of his superiority. Hiding beneath this shimmering glow, however, lay a base malice. Christians who stood in danger of falling under Ottoman dominion were therefore to be warned emphatically about these threats and equipped with the iron ration of catechetical knowledge to survive them.[126]

From their work on the apocalyptic portions of the book of Daniel in 1529, Luther and his colleagues Jonas and Melanchthon gained new insight into the Ottoman Empire. Thereafter the book of Daniel would remain an important witness for Wittenberg's theological-historical thinking. Like some ancient church fathers, Luther interpreted the four beasts named in Daniel 7 as the empires of the Assyrians, the Babylonians and Persians, Alexander the Great and his Hellenistic successors, and finally the Romans. For Luther, as for most of his contemporaries, his own time was lodged in the framework of the fourth and final world empire, the *imperium Romanum*, which at the time of Charlemagne had been renewed and transferred to the West. The fourth beast had ten horns, which Luther identified as kingdoms within the Roman Empire. Beneath the tenth horn, according to Daniel 7, an eleventh arises that casts away three of the other horns: this represents the empire of Muhammad swallowing up Egypt, Asia Minor, and Greece.[127] Luther's interpretation got down into individual details in the biblical text; the snout that carried the horn perhaps signified the "gruesome blasphemies, with which Mohammed completely abolishes Christ" and places himself over him.[128]

Because Luther had located the most current and threatening enemy of Christianity, "the Turks," in the Bible, he became even more convinced that the end of history and the final judgment stood immediately at the door. Christianity, in the time left, would be exposed to sorrow and affliction in order to endure until the end with a courageous witness to its Lord, to confess the gospel, and to enter eternal life as a "holy remnant." Even when Luther no longer expected Christ's return in judgment in his own lifetime, he still hoped that the Lord would shorten his church's time of suffering. He firmly counted on the end of history coming within the next decade. Next to the Apocalypse of John, the prophecy of Daniel became the most important biblical book to help him formulate a chronological table that appeared in print in 1544 as *Supputatio annorum mundi* (*Reckoning the Years of the World*).[129] Therein he proceeded on the assumption that the year 1540 was the 5,500th year since the creation of the world. Luther agreed with the tradition that expected the world to last six thousand years in all, but thought God would cut that short for the sake of his righteous ones.

A prophecy of the Franciscan John Hilten that evidently made an especially lasting impression on Luther predicted the complete destruction of Germany at the hands of the Ottoman Empire in 1600.[130] Luther wrote this in chalk on the wall of his study, yet still hoped that the last judgment would come earlier to bring this suffering to an end. Even after the end of the Reformation proper, Lutherans in Germany persisted in marked end-time expectations until after the Thirty Years' War. These would flare up and agitate people, time and again—another part of Luther's legacy.

As for the Jews, Luther used New Testament language; they were "a brood of vipers," "children of the devil." His enmity for them became increasingly obsessive, climaxing in his late years. This was the dark obverse of his love for Christ, his faith in justification, and his interpretation of Scripture. Because Luther was thoroughly convinced that the Old Testament announced Jesus Christ as Messiah and could be rightly understood by faith in Christ alone, to deny the messianic prophecies of the Old Testament amounted to a betrayal of Christ and the loss of the certainty of salvation. That makes Luther's anti-Semitism—which had plenty of company in early modern times—no unimportant side note in his theology. During the early Reformation Luther tended to lead Christians to the suffering Christ as the one and only basis for their salvation, and lead them away from the widespread abuse of the passion of Christ against the Jews.[131] His later writings, by contrast, were suffused with the idea that the Jews unceasingly reviled Christ in their worship and tried to harm Christian believers.

Amid the euphoria of the early 1520s, Luther thought it well possible that a Jewish conversion of note might come since now, for the first time in centuries, Jews could hear preached the unadulterated gospel. This hope turned to hatred of immoderate proportions for a number of reasons. The defenders of the pope's church reviled Luther and his followers as "Jew lovers" to discredit them. The mission of Jewish evangelization met no success. The polemical writings of Jews who did not convert strengthened Luther's belief in Jewish hardness of heart and unremitting enmity toward Christ. It also induced him to distort Jewish faith practices.

The final straw came from Christian studies of Hebrew that relativized his interpretation of the Old Testament's messianic witness with historical-philological arguments. In the end, he felt expelling the Jews from Protestant cities and territories to be a most sacred obligation.

For Luther the Jews epitomized a failed relationship with God, in which believers tried to attain righteousness through their own works of the law. This connected the Jews to "the papists," "the Turks," and the "Enthusiasts" in his own camp. The demonic element among the Jews, however, was worse than that among these other foes of Christ, for Jews had possessed the witness of the Messiah Jesus, only to misunderstand it to their guilt. Luther could explain this misunderstanding only by the theory that God had hardened their hearts to demonstrate by the history of their suffering where the denial of the true Messiah led, namely, to an unstable, flight-filled, threatened life culminating in rejection by God and humanity.

From the voices of Luther's Jewish contemporaries, it is clear that they saw a strong contrast between the "young" and the "old" Reformer, above all, between the Luther of 1523 (*That Jesus Christ Was Born a Jew*)[132] and the Luther of 1543 (*On the Jews and Their Lies*).[133] As for Luther's concrete political suggestions, we cannot overlook that he moved from contemplating a policy of limited toleration for a fixed time to the traditional stance of expulsion. His theological assessment of Judaism, however, showed no change at all. In no phase of his life was it credited as a bearer of divine promise; it was seen only as an antiquated religion that had been annulled by God, a piety of human self-justification that dishonored Christ.

Among the numerous manifestations of the devil were the "false teachers" with whom Luther occupied himself with special intensity. The "pig theologians" out of the pope's church were in his eyes as much the servants of the devil as the apostates from his own camp who in his judgment falsified the Scripture. Luther's opponents, both those on the "right" and those on the "left," had in common that they placed their own opinions, rational arguments, or ecclesiastical traditions above the witness of Scripture. "Dreaming" or "enthusiasm" for Luther described every form of human and religious autonomy that did not allow itself to be led in thought and deed by the manifest Word of Christ in Scripture, but followed its own discretion and subjective conviction. Luther's certainty of faith did not permit plural interpretations of the biblical witness on questions that involved Christian salvation. If he detected indifference or human rationality in operation against the clear witness of Scripture as he understood it, then the devil had to be at work. For the devil, according to Luther, squeezes himself between God and human beings with the single goal of undermining faith in the Word.

It is this passion, of upholding faith in the Word against any interpretation that smacked of rationalism, that explains Luther's stand for the traditional wording of the communion service in his controversy with Karlstadt, Zwingli, and various other Swiss and upper German theologians. The idea that Christ was bodily present in the bread and wine might contradict all human reasoning, but that, he insisted, was no reason to weaken or reduce the offensiveness of the clear word of Scripture. The latter simply and explicitly reads: "This is my body," and may not be interpreted to mean "this represents my body" or "this is a sign of my body" or something similar. At the Religious Colloquy in Marburg of 1529, Luther boldly took chalk and wrote Christ's words of institution on the table to settle the controversy. These for him set the bounds and plumb line for any agreement or common understanding. In the presence of the Word of Christ, faith alone was the appropriate attitude. Reason served as the "devil's whore," placing itself over the Word, disrupting faith and the certainty of salvation, thus achieving the devil's goal.

Christians in real life encounter the devil as a living power and in a variety of real-world incarnations, Luther taught. Sorrow and grief constitute one of his weapons, wielded against sensitive individuals to drive them into isolation and despair. Loneliness too leaves one vulnerable and defenseless against the devil's onslaughts. The devil also steps up as an apostle of morals who tries to give us a bad conscience over the littlest things: eating, or drinking, or whatever involves the human need for togetherness. So Luther comforted his pupil Jerome Weller, who lived in his house fellowship and was responsible for educating his children, when he was brought down by the assaults of the devil. In a letter sent from Coburg Fortress during the Augsburg Imperial Diet of 1530, Luther recommended that Weller scorn the devil by kicking over the traces. Drink a lot, joke, play, and in a soberly way commit little sins.[134] Precisely when the devil fights with us over things that are nothing and perhaps says: "'Don't drink,' you should answer him: 'That's precisely why I will drink, because you forbid it; I will even drink a lot.'"[135]

The freedom of faith, according to Luther, creates a wholesome distance over against anything that enslaves people; Christians open a sovereign association with the things of this world because they know that the death sentence hanging over them as sinners has been annulled by the suffering of the Son of God. Eating, drinking, conversation, even thoughts about women can drive away depression or despair;[136] this Luther knew from his own experience. In the long run, however, strategies of this kind would not fend off the cold sweat of fear triggered by the demonic assaults that visited the heretic at night, even with his wife by his side.[137]

The devil, who argued with him and wanted to bring him to recant, who indeed slept with him more than his wife did,[138] would not be diverted even during sex: "I have often grabbed my Katie's B and Z [*Brüste und Zitze*: breasts and nipples] but the evil thoughts did not go away [*nec abire malae cogitationes*]."[139] In the end, the only thing that remained for Luther was that which stood at the beginning and with which everything had started: "I have the *verbum* [Word] and let that suffice."[140]

For Luther human life proceeded in the midst of sin, death, and the fear of the devil and of hell. His own experience was no exception on this score but represented what really mattered: "In the midst of life, we are surrounded by death."[141] Those are the words he used in reworking the Latin antiphon "Media vita in morte sumus." For this completely "medieval" understanding of human wretchedness, Luther found an answer that, in its pointed exclusivity and one-sidedness, was no longer "medieval": "Where can we flee, where will we be able to stay? / To you, Lord Christ, alone. / ... Holy merciful Savior, / You, eternal God, / From true faith's comfort let us not fall away."[142]

Whoever loves Christ must scorn whatever fights against him as the devil's work. In both love and scorn, Luther was great.

Luther and Christianity

In the history of the Western Church—indeed, of Christianity as a whole—the Lutheran Reformation marks a radical break. This holds for theological understanding, for the practice of faith, and for the institutional form of ecclesiastical fellowship. Luther's work has not only continued to influence those who implicitly or explicitly follow him in the so-called Lutheran church bodies. The Anabaptists and the spiritualists had to work out their own type of religious communities in connection with or by differentiation from him. Likewise, in the Reformation movement that proceeded from him, the pope's church for the first time found itself opposed to a massive heresy that it could neither assimilate nor eliminate, and whose questions posed a challenge from which, in the long run, it could not escape. From its controversy with Luther and all its consequences, Rome too at last became a different church. Its fundamental renewal, which was begun and propelled by the Council of Trent (1545–1563), brought forth the Roman Catholic confessional church, which still today represents itself as the legally and organizationally strongest, and most truly global, form of institutional Christianity.

Through Luther and the conditions that enabled the Reformation to stay alive, a church without the pope became a reality in the domain of Western Christianity. Luther sometimes characterized the primary achievement of his life as a fight against the papacy. For example, as an inscription on his grave he considered the prophetic statement that, alive, he would ruin the pope; dead, he would be the pope's death (*Pestis eram vivens, moriens ero mors tua, papa*).[1] Obviously, that expectation did not come true. Nevertheless, with Luther churchly Christianity became plural, not because he had wanted this, but because in the long run the pope's church closed itself off to his questions. For the condemnation of this "heretic" has not yet been revoked even today; according to Roman Catholic teaching, Luther is damned for time and eternity. The condemnation applies not only to Luther himself but also to all those who might feel committed, directly or indirectly, to his interpretation of Christianity.

Being condemned as a heretic while attesting that he was bound by conscience to Holy Scripture and, in his judgment, had never been refuted on that score, was Luther's traumatic primal experience and the birth shock of Protestant Christianity. Ejected from the protective lap of mother church, the church of Luther could not be a mother; "the church is a daughter, born from the Word, not a mother of the Word" (*Ecclesia enim est filia, nata ex verbo, non est mater verbi*).[2] The freedom of the church Luther derived from its freedom for the gospel and for faith. His rejection of individualistic and sectarian forms of Christian community was based on the pathos of freedom that he saw God opening up in accepting sinners—who cannot look away from the self, and cannot love God and neighbor for their own sake—for the sake of Christ, by grace alone. Such a freedom, bestowed as a gift of God and made known through the Word, should not fall into the hands of just any person or religious collective. That is why God sustains a church that is empowered to speak in the authority of freedom. From Luther's perspective, the Anabaptist and spiritualist sects reproduced the same compulsion of conscience exercised by the pope's church, from which he himself had just escaped. Thus, connection with or membership in the church was never an end in itself for Luther, as it was in the alternative ecclesiastical communions formed on the "left wing" of Protestantism. Rather, the church exists to provide a good conscience before God, to make faith possible. As a fellowship whose very nature consists in making itself superfluous ever and anon, the church of the gospel as Luther conceived of it is a new kind of institutional phenomenon in the history of Christianity.

The freedom from the conscience-binding yoke of the pope's church was possible during and after the Reformation only because the civil authorities filled in the vacuum of power created by the abolition of the canon law with all its legislative, regulatory, and disciplinary details. This civil absorption of religion had already started before the Reformation in countries that asserted sovereign authority over the church. It continued on after the Reformation in Catholic states, but proceeded further under Protestantism insofar as the latter granted politically responsible laity the right to define Christian teaching in a binding way under the principle of the priesthood of all believers. Even if the civil authorities, as a rule, took the advice of their theologians on such matters, still an epochal shift in the history of Christianity occurred in that political sovereigns could determine the religious confession of their subjects. This gave the Lutheran churches in Germany a special proximity to the state that still holds today; it has encouraged a mentality by which people might relate to Christianity in a thoroughly positive way, yet take care to keep a safe distance from the visible church institution. The ambivalence with which evangelical Christians both connect with and distance themselves from their church has theological roots in Luther's understanding of the church, but also in historical reasons that stem from the restructuring of the church after the sixteenth century, in conditions that Luther could hardly have influenced.

Luther understood his condemnation of the pope's church to be a necessary consequence of the gospel itself. Under the pope, he said, "we knew absolutely nothing that a Christian ought to know."[3] Now, however, "our Gospel," to which we came "blindly and by pure chance,"[4] has "accomplished much good."[5] Indeed, it made possible for the first time a relevant knowledge of God and the world in general: "What Christ is," and baptism, and faith, and comfort, and civil authority, and marriage, and the church, and a Christian, and the cross,[6] had now become known for the first time through him, "the prophet of the Germans"[7]—that is to say, by Christ working through him. It is no wonder that this astounding claim could not possibly be integrated into the established church, for it meant that the whole development of the Western Church for almost a thousand years was fatally false. Not to have declared Luther a heretic would have meant giving up Rome's claim to universality and truth.

Where did Luther, who was inclined to the sharpest polemics, receive this unbounded, and in psychological perspective nearly unfathomable, truth claim? From being a Christian, from his faith, from his very consciousness of God. In his controversy with Erasmus of Rotterdam, when Luther railed against this religious intellectual who seemed inclined to skepticism and indifference, the man from Wittenberg etched what makes a Christian in bold relief. A Christian speaks in the confessional mode or in *assertiones,*[8] binding theological statements; he depends unchangeably, unyieldingly, and insurmountably on the truth of God. To annul such assertions meant annulling Christianity itself (*tolle assertiones, et christianismum tulisti*).[9] Precisely that happens, however, when—as in Erasmus—the question of whether human beings can do something to earn God's mercy by the strength of their own will is handled as a needless or ambiguous matter. A form of Christianity (*forma Christianismi*)[10] that teaches us to strive with all our strength and submit ourselves to church penance as the means of earning the mercy of the Lord fixates us upon ourselves and leaves us in the crisis of conscience where the ever-striving, ever-troubled monk had begun. The single and highest comfort of the Christian, instead, is the certainty that God steadfastly desires the salvation and life of his creatures, that God does not lie, and that God has said this inviolably in his Word, once and for all.[11]

God's will to save is revealed in Christ, the one divine-human Person in two natures. In contrast to the previous history of dogma and to his contemporary critics both "right" and "left," this doctrine for Luther proved to be living and life-giving. These others had passed along or relativized the two-natures teaching as "dogmatically correct," or as a metaphysical theory to be taught but not examined, or as a faith statement opaque to natural reason. But Christ's being truly God and truly a human being Luther made directly relevant to people's salvation in a creative theological way. For Luther the unique relationship between God, who really participates in suffering in the person of Christ, and the human being, who in Christ shares in the perfect nature of God, defined God's relationship to humanity as a whole in a new saving way. From the communion between God and human in Christ it was no longer appropriate to define God as a human being–less, inhuman Lord, or human beings as dependent creatures locked into themselves. In Christ the free God and the freed human being, the Creator and creature, the most extreme opposites are thus reconciled in the closest communion. As Luther put it in a Christmas song he composed in 1524: "The Son of the Father by nature God, / lived as a guest in earth's abode / and leads us out of this vale of tears and strife / and makes us heirs of eternal life. / *kyrieleis*" (Lord, have mercy!).[12] In faith, human beings participate in the reality of God, founding their being, nature, and authenticity, which they have been liberated to realize, in the "ex-centric" person Jesus Christ.

Luther's faith lay in this certainty, and in it he grounded Christianity. His formulas of what it meant to be called a Christian were more pregnant with meaning than probably any other before: "To be a Christian is to have the Gospel and believe in Christ. This faith brings forgiveness of sins and God's grace. It comes, however, only from the Holy Spirit, who engenders this faith through the Word, without our doing anything in addition or working along with it. It is God's own work."[13]

If it is true that to have a religion means "to have something upon which the heart completely trusts,"[14] then Martin Luther unlocked religion for Christianity, and for the world.

In this translation the references that the author placed in the text, citing the "Weimar Edition" (WA) of Luther's works, have been put in endnotes. Unless they are only available in the Weimar Edition, the translator has added references to the American Edition (cited as *LW = Luther's Works*). The English translation of Luther's words follows *LW*, slightly adapted, but the references also cite the places where they can be found in their original language.

AWA   *Archiv zur Weimarer Ausgabe.* Cölogne: H. Bohlau,
         1981.
LW   *Luther's Works.* Edited by Jaroslav Pelikan and
         Helmut T. Lehmann. 55 vols. St. Louis: Concordia;
         Philadelphia: Fortress, 1955–1986.
WA   D. *Martin Luthers Werke: Kritische Gesamtausgabe.*
         65 vols. Weimar: Hermann Böhlaus Nachfolger,
         1883–1985.
WABr   D. *Martin Luthers Werke: Kritische Gesamtausgabe,*
         Briefwechsel. 18 vols. Weimar: Hermann Böhlaus
         Nachfolger, 1930–1985.
WADB   D. *Martin Luthers Werke: Kritische Gesamtausgabe,*
         Deutsche Bibel. 12 vols. Weimar: Hermann Böhlaus
         Nachfolger, 1906–1961.
WATr   D. *Martin Luthers Werke: Kritische Gesamtausgabe,*
         Tischreden. 6 vols. Weimar: Hermann Böhlaus Na-
         chfolger, 1912–1921.

Introduction

1 B. Moeller, K. Stackmann, Luder—Luther—Eleutherius: Er-
wägungen zu Luthers Namen (Göttingen: Vandenhoeck and
Ruprecht, 1981).

2 Homiletical guides for Gospel and Epistle passages assigned
for the church year.

The Search for Martin Luther

1 WA 18:786.25f.; *LW* 33:294.

2 WA 48:241; WATr 5:168.35; 318.2f.; *LW* 54:476; WABr
12:363f.

3 WABr 9:573.59–69; *LW* 34:297.

4 WABr 1:122.56f. See Preserved Smith, *Luther's Correspon-
dence and Other Contemporary Letters*, vol. 1 (Philadelphia:
Lutheran Publication Society, 1913), 64.

5 WABr 2:455.41f.; in the letter to Elector Frederick of Saxony,
March 5, 1522. *LW* 48:390.

6 Cf. WA 30 II:635.4–636.10; *LW* 35:186.

7 WA 2:451.25f.: *sanctissima . . . superbia*; cf. 471.30; *LW*
27:162; cf. 192–93; WA 25:12.21; *LW* 29:11.

8 WA 30 III:366.8; *LW* 34:91.

9 WA 15:216.4f.; *LW* 40:55.

10 WA 7:313.17; *LW* 32:9.

11 WA 7:313.21–23; *LW* 32:9.

12 (WA 8:482.32–483.3); *LW* 36:134.

13 WATr 5:23.27–24.6.

14 WATr 1:69.21–24.

15 WABr 5:162.3–12; WA 50:601.5f.; *LW* 41:110f.

16 Isa. 62:1 (WA 15:27.12–21); *LW* 45:347–48.

17 WA 15:27.28f.; *LW* 45:348.

18 WA 30 III:290.28; *LW* 47:29.

19 WA 15:28.1f.; *LW* 45:348.

20 WA 9:303.17ff.; *LW* 45:70.

21 WA 8:684.26–29.

22 WA 17 I:232.2f.; *LW* 12:186.

23 See WA 56:480.5–7; *LW* 25:472; WA 30 III:437.18f.

24 WA 6:404.31–405.1; *LW* 44:124.

25 WABr 2:254.53–255.54; *LW* 48:196–97; cf. WA 7:162.8–15; cf. *LW* 31:383.

26 WA 10 II:106.10f.; *LW* 39:248f.

27 WA 30 II:635.8–636.2; *LW* 35:185–86.

28 WA 30 III:386.14–387.2; *LW* 34:103.

29 WA 10 II:105.17f., 19f.; *LW* 39:247.

30 WA 7:164.5f.; *LW* 31:384.

31 WA 10 II:106.2; *LW* 39:248; cf. WATr 2:307.33–35.

32 WA 7:162.8; *LW* 31:383.

33 WA 30 II:636.2f.; *LW* 35:187.

34 WA 8:685.6ff.; *LW* 45:70; cf. WA 10 II:40.5–29; *LW* 36:265.

35 WA 6:404.23ff.; 405.2; *LW* 44:123–24.

36 By Erasmus's publisher, Froben of Basel, 1518.

37 2 Kings 2:11.

38 WA 10 I.1:148.14f.

39 WABr 7:329.18.

40 WA 8:683.24f.; *LW* 45:67–68.

41 Cf., e.g., WABr 2:305.17; cf. 48:201–3.

42 WA 8:685.4–15; *LW* 45:70–71.

Living in the Reformation of God

1   WA 1:629.27–31.
2   WA 50:195.18–23.
3   WA 38:271.3; *LW* 38:231.
4   WABr 1:13f.
5   WA 49:322.12f.
6   WATr 4:440.9f.
7   WA 8:573.24; *LW* 48:331.
8   Acts 9:3; 22:6; 26:13.
9   WATr 4:440.14ff.
10 *Baccalaureus biblicus.*
11 *Baccalaureus sententiarius.*
12 WA 1:378.21–23; *LW* 31:75.
13 See his marginal glosses in WA 9:2–27 and WA 9:28–94.
14 WA 54:179–87; *LW* 34:327–38.
15 Rom. 1:17b; Hab. 2:4.
16 WA 1:224–28; *LW* 31:9–16.
17 WABr 1:107.22–24.
18 Saxony had been divided in 1485 between the two sons of the House of Wettin, the older Ernest and the younger Albert. The power to participate in the election of the Holy Roman emperor went with the Ernestine line; hence these rulers were titled elector, and their lands Electoral Saxony. On the Albertine side these were duke and duchy. [JB]
19 Matt. 4:17.
20 WA 1:233.10f.; *LW* 31:25.
21 WA 1:229–38; *LW* 31:25–33.
22 WA 1:239–46.
23 WA 1:233.23f.; *LW* 31:26; WA 1:539.32–545.8; *LW* 31:98–107.
24 If the decrees were wrong, Luther must agree with the condemned positions. [JB]
25 WA 6:353–78; *LW* 35:79–111; WA 6:497–573; *LW* 36:126.

26 WA 6:285–324; *LW* 39:55–104.

27 WA 6:404–69; *LW* 44:123–217.

28 WA 7:20–38, Latin, 42–73; *LW* 31:333–77.

29 WA 6:202–76; *LW* 44:21–114.

30 WABr 2:295.17–19.

31 WA 8:573–669; *LW* 44:251–400.

32 WA 10 I.1; 10 I.2; *LW* 52.

33 2 Cor. 12:7.

34 WA 54:191–94; *LW* 34:365–66.

35 WA 54:193.2; *LW* 34:365.

A Theological Life

1 WA 54:179.31–33; *LW* 34:328.

2 *Antilogiam,* WA 54:180.1; *LW* 34:328.

3 WA 50:657.5–11; *LW* 34:283–84.

4 WA 54:179.15–18; *LW* 34:328.

5 WA 50:658.7f.; *LW* 34:284.

6 *Dreckret und Dreckretals. Dreck* in German means dirt.

7 WA 50:658.14–20; *LW* 34:285.

8 WA 54:179.6f.; *LW* 34:327.

9 WA 30 I:125–238.

10 WA 18:600–787; *LW* 33:3–295.

11 WATr 3:623.7; *LW* 54:274–75.

12 1 Cor. 1:18.

13 WA 50:659.4; *LW* 34:285f.

14 WA 50:659.5–7; *LW* 34:285.

15 WA 50:659.7; *LW* 34:285.

16 WA 50:659.22–24; *LW* 34:286.

17 WA 50:659.33; *LW* 34:286.

18 WA 50:660.9; *LW* 34:287.

19 WA 50:660.9, 2–4; *LW* 34:285–87.

20 An extraordinarily expensive commodity at the time.

21 WA 50:660.10–14; *LW* 34:287.

22 WA 50:657–61; *LW* 34:283–88.

23 WA 45:599.9–15; *LW* 24:151.

24 WA 7:550.1–552.4; *LW* 21:302–4.

25 WA 10 III:426.18–23.

26 WA 23:36.25f.

27 WA 48:241f.

28 WATr 1:16.13; *LW* 54:7.

29 WATr 3:598.10; 5:75.10; 1:44.16–20; *LW* 54:13–14.

30 WATr 1:44.18–20; *LW* 54:13.

31 WATr 5:75.14.

32 WATr 1:44.23f.; *LW* 54:14f.

33 WATr 3:598.14.

34 WATr 1, no. 116; *LW* 54:13–14, no. 116.

35 WABr 1:171.72f.

36 WATr 2:6.1–3; *LW* 54:127–28.

37 WATr 2:244.20–23; *LW* 54:165.

38 WA 7:834.4–9; *LW* 32:112; WA 876.11–877.6.

39 WADB 6:24.

40 WA 17 I:513.11.

41 WADB 6:3.23–25; *LW* 35:358.

42 WADB 6:8.16–20; *LW* 35:360–61.

43 WADB 6:4.17–20; *LW* 35:358–59.

44 WADB 6:10.12; *LW* 35:361–62.

45 WADB 6:10.34; *LW* 35:362.

46 WA 48:448.2–6; WATr 1:487.11f.; WADB 6:xxxii; WABr 2:413.6f.; *LW* 48:356–57.

47 Joel 3.

48 WA 30 II:640; *LW* 35:194–95.

49 WATr 2:439.12, no. 2381.

50 WATr 2:40.19–22; *LW* 54:135–36.

51 WADB 12:2f.

52 WADB 3 and 4.

53 WA 30 II:636.17f.; *LW* 35:188.

54 WA 30 II:635.11–24; *LW* 35:185–86; WA 30 II:640.18; *LW* 35:194; WA 30 II:633.24f.; *LW* 35:183.

55 WA 30 II:640.5; *LW* 35:193.

56 WA 30 II:633.14; *LW* 35:182. Scholars wrote in Latin in those days, while Luther started writing about intellectual and theological subjects in German.

57 WA 30 II:640.30f.; *LW* 35:194.

58 WA 30 II:637.17–22; *LW* 35:189.

59 WA 7:97.23.

60 WA 18:606.24–31; *LW* 33:25–26.

61 WA 30 II:635.21f.; *LW* 35:186.

62 WA 7:161.8–162.1; *LW* 31:383–84.

63 WA 10 III:10; *LW* 51:73–74.

64 WA 1:60–141 (mostly sermons of 1514), 398–521.

65 H. Dannenbauer, *Luther als religiöser Volksschriftsteller* (Tübingen: J. C. B. Mohr, 1930).

66 WA 12:142.8–12; *LW* 28:56.

67 WATr 2:669.12.

68 WA 15:342.8.

69 WA 15:345.12–14.

70 WATr 4:412.35; *LW* 54:358–59.

71 Josh. 10:12.

72 WATr 3:627.11; *LW* 54:277, no. 3801.

73 Cited according to WABr 9:236.

74 WATr 4:564.21–565.1.

75 WA 48:201.5.

76 WA 18:605.20f.; *LW* 33:23–24.

77 WA 30 I:133.2f.

78 WA 26:339.33–36, 39; 340.2; *LW* 37:227–28.

79 WA 8:573–669; *LW* 44:251–400.

80 WA 18:291–334; *LW* 46:17–43.

81 WATr 5:657.14–18.

82 WA 18:357–61; *LW* 46:49–55.

83 WA 18:384–401; *LW* 46:63–85.

84 WA 18:400.24; *LW* 46:84.

85 WA 18:400.36; *LW* 46:84.

86 WA 6:404–69; *LW* 44:123–217.

87 *On Temporal Authority*: WA 11:245–81; *LW* 45:81–129; *Whether Soldiers, Too, Can Be Saved*: WA 19:623–62; *LW* 46:93–137.

88 Cf. WA 23:282.28ff.; *LW* 37:149f.

89 WATr 1:195.19.

90 WA 38.358–75; *LW* 43:193–211.

91 WA 30 I:365ff.

92 WABr 2:354.27; cf. *LW* 48:255.

93 WABr 2:454.24; *LW* 48:389.

94 Gal. 1:11–12.

95 WABr 2:455.41f.; *LW* 48:390.

96 WABr 3:394.22f.; *LW* 49:93.

97 WABr 3:549.11; WATr 4:602.2; *LW* 54:374; 641.11; WABr 5:7.2.

98 WABr 3:549.10–12.

99 WABr 3:541.8.

100 Hos. 1.

101 WABr 4:11, 41–49.

102 WA 50:250.3.

103 WA 49:600.14; *LW* 51:343.

104 WA 18:652.23; *LW* 33:89.

105 WA 19:72–113.669; *LW* 53:61–90.

106 WA 19:72.19; *LW* 53:61.

107 WA 19:72.18, 23; *LW* 53:61.

108 WA 19:72.27f.; *LW* 53:61.

109 WA 19:75.3.5; *LW* 53:64.

110 *AWA* 4:236f. *Lutheran Book of Worship*, no. 308, has "God the Father, Be our Stay," which I changed to make it closer to the German in what is mostly my translation.

111 *AWA* 4:196. The words taken from *Evangelical Lutheran Worship* (Minneapolis: Augsburg Fortress, 2006), no. 370.

112 *AWA* 4:154; *Evangelical Lutheran Worship*, no. 595.

113 *AWA* 4:304.

114 WA 54:206–99; *LW* 41:263–376.

115 2 Thess. 2:4; Dan. 11:31, 36; 9:27; Matt. 24:15.

116 WABr 9:175.17.

117 WA 30 II:107–48; *LW* 46:161–205.

118 WA 30 II:160–97.

119 WADB 11/II:2–130.

120 WA 1:535.35–39; *LW* 31:92.

121 WA 30 II:122.2–11; *LW* 46:176–77.

122 WA 30 II:123.35; *LW* 46:178.

123 WA 30 II:126.1f.; *LW* 46:181.

124 2 Cor. 11:14.

125 WA 30 II:128.22–25; *LW* 46:183.

126 WA 30 II:186.1–14.

127 WA 30 II:164.4–167.12.

128 WA 30 II:168.24–26.

129 WA 53:1–184.

130 WA 48:284 [to 133f.].

131 WA 2:136.3–10; *LW* 42:7.

132 WA 11:314–36; *LW* 45:199–229.

133 WA 53:417–552; *LW* 47:137–306.

134 WABr 5:518, no.1670. Philip Krey and Peter Krey, *Luther's Spirituality* (New York: Paulist, 2007), 8–10.

135 WABr 5:519.48–51; Krey and Krey, *Luther's Spirituality,* 9.

136 WATr 1:49.27ff.; *LW* 54:15–18.

137 WATr 1:210.2–4; 232.32f.; *LW* 54:89–90.

138 WATr 1:289.7–9.

139 WATr 1:406.22–24.

140 WATr 1:232.33f.; *LW* 54:89–90.

141 *AWA* 4:160.

142 *AWA* 4:161.

Epilogue

1   WATr 3:390.18; *LW* 54:227; cf. WA 30 III:279.18f.; *LW* 47:15–16 and more often.

2   WA 42:334.12; *LW* 2:101.

3   WA 30 III:317.23f.; *LW* 47:52.

4   WADB 11/II:105.11.

5   WA 30 III:317.15; *LW* 47:52.

6   WA 30 III:317.16–23; *LW* 47:52.

7   WA 30 III:290.28; *LW* 47:29.

8   WA 18:603.12; *LW* 33:20.

9   WA 18:603.28f.; *LW* 33:21.

10   WA 18:611.1; *LW* 33:30–31.

11   WA 18:618.22–619.15; *LW* 33:42–43.

12   *AWA* 4:166.

13   WATr 3:279.28–31.

14   WA 30 I:139.5f.

Disputation of Doctor Martin Luther
on the Power and Efficacy of Indulgences

October 31, 1517

Out of love for the truth and the desire to bring it to light, the following propositions will be discussed at Wittenberg, under the presidency of the Reverend Father Martin Luther, Master of Arts and of Sacred Theology, and Lecturer in Ordinary on the same at that place. Wherefore he requests that those who are unable to be present and debate orally with us, may do so by letter.

In the Name of our Lord Jesus Christ. Amen.

1. Our Lord and Master Jesus Christ, when He said "repent," willed that the whole life of believers should be repentance.

2. This word cannot be understood to mean sacramental penance, i.e., confession and satisfaction, which is administered by the priests.

3. Yet it means not inward repentance only; nay, there is no inward repentance which does not outwardly work diverse mortifications of the flesh.

4. The penalty [of sin], therefore, continues so long as hatred of self continues; for this is the true inward repentance, and continues until our entrance into the kingdom of heaven.

5. The pope does not intend to remit, and cannot remit any penalties other than those which he has imposed either by his own authority or by that of the Canons.

6. The pope cannot remit any guilt, except by declaring that it has been remitted by God and by assenting to God's remission; though, to be sure, he may grant remission in cases reserved to his judgment. If his right to grant remission in such cases were despised, the guilt would remain entirely unforgiven.

7. God remits guilt to no one whom He does not, at the same time, humble in all things and bring into subjection to His vicar, the priest.

8. The penitential canons are imposed only on the living, and, according to them, nothing should be imposed on the dying.

9. Therefore the Holy Spirit in the pope is kind to us, because in his decrees he always makes exception of the article of death and of necessity.

10. Ignorant and wicked are the doings of those priests who, in the case of the dying, reserve canonical penances for purgatory.

11. This changing of the canonical penalty to the penalty of purgatory is quite evidently one of the tares that were sown while the bishops slept.

12. In former times the canonical penalties were imposed not after, but before absolution, as tests of true contrition.

13. The dying are freed by death from all penalties; they are already dead to canonical rules, and have a right to be released from them.

14. The imperfect health [of soul], that is to say, the imperfect love, of the dying brings with it, of necessity, great fear; and the smaller the love, the greater is the fear.

15. This fear and horror is sufficient of itself alone (to say nothing of other things) to constitute the penalty of purgatory, since it is very near to the horror of despair.

16. Hell, purgatory, and heaven seem to differ as do despair, almost-despair, and the assurance of safety.

17. With souls in purgatory it seems necessary that horror should grow less and love increase.

18. It seems unproved, either by reason or Scripture, that they are outside the state of merit, that is to say, of increasing love.

19. Again, it seems unproved that they, or at least that all of them, are certain or assured of their own blessedness, though we may be quite certain of it.

20. Therefore by "full remission of all penalties" the pope means not actually "of all," but only of those imposed by himself.

21. Therefore those preachers of indulgences are in error, who say that by the pope's indulgences a man is freed from every penalty, and saved;

22. Whereas he remits to souls in purgatory no penalty which, according to the canons, they would have had to pay in this life.

23. If it is at all possible to grant to any one the remission of all penalties whatsoever, it is certain that this remission can be granted only to the most perfect, that is, to the very fewest.

24. It must needs be, therefore, that the greater part of the people are deceived by that indiscriminate and highsounding promise of release from penalty.

25. The power which the pope has, in a general way, over purgatory, is just like the power which any bishop or curate has, in a special way, within his own diocese or parish.

26. The pope does well when he grants remission to souls [in purgatory], not by the power of the keys (which he does not possess), but by way of intercession.

27. They preach human doctrines who say that so soon as the penny jingles into the money-box, the soul flies out [of purgatory].

28. It is certain that when the penny jingles into the money-box, gain and avarice can be increased, but the result of the intercession of the Church is in the power of God alone.

29. Who knows whether all the souls in purgatory wish to be bought out of it, as in the legend of Sts. Severinus and Paschal.

30. No one is sure that his own contrition is sincere; much less that he has attained full remission.

31. Rare as is the man that is truly penitent, so rare is also the man who truly buys indulgences, i.e., such men are most rare.

32. They will be condemned eternally, together with their teachers, who believe themselves sure of their salvation because they have letters of pardon.

33. Men must be on their guard against those who say that the pope's pardons are that inestimable gift of God by which man is reconciled to Him;

34. For these "graces of pardon" concern only the penalties of sacramental satisfaction, and these are appointed by man.

35. They preach no Christian doctrine who teach that contrition is not necessary in those who intend to buy souls out of purgatory or to buy confessionalia.

36. Every truly repentant Christian has a right to full remission of penalty and guilt, even without letters of pardon.

37. Every true Christian, whether living or dead, has part in all the blessings of Christ and the Church; and this is granted him by God, even without letters of pardon.

38. Nevertheless, the remission and participation [in the blessings of the Church] which are granted by the pope are in no way to be despised, for they are, as I have said, the declaration of divine remission.

39. It is most difficult, even for the very keenest theologians, at one and the same time to commend to the people the abundance of pardons and [the need of] true contrition.

40. True contrition seeks and loves penalties, but liberal pardons only relax penalties and cause them to be hated, or at least, furnish an occasion [for hating them].

41. Apostolic pardons are to be preached with caution, lest the people may falsely think them preferable to other good works of love.

42. Christians are to be taught that the pope does not intend the buying of pardons to be compared in any way to works of mercy.

43. Christians are to be taught that he who gives to the poor or lends to the needy does a better work than buying pardons;

44. Because love grows by works of love, and man becomes better; but by pardons man does not grow better, only more free from penalty.

45. Christians are to be taught that he who sees a man in need, and passes him by, and gives [his money] for pardons, purchases not the indulgences of the pope, but the indignation of God.

46. Christians are to be taught that unless they have more than they need, they are bound to keep back what is necessary for their own families, and by no means to squander it on pardons.

47. Christians are to be taught that the buying of pardons is a matter of free will, and not of commandment.

48. Christians are to be taught that the pope, in granting pardons, needs, and therefore desires, their devout prayer for him more than the money they bring.

49. Christians are to be taught that the pope's pardons are useful, if they do not put their trust in them; but altogether harmful, if through them they lose their fear of God.

50. Christians are to be taught that if the pope knew the exactions of the pardon-preachers, he would rather that St. Peter's church should go to ashes, than that it should be built up with the skin, flesh and bones of his sheep.

51. Christians are to be taught that it would be the pope's wish, as it is his duty, to give of his own money to very many of those from whom certain hawkers of pardons cajole money, even though the church of St. Peter might have to be sold.

52. The assurance of salvation by letters of pardon is vain, even though the commissary, nay, even though the pope himself, were to stake his soul upon it.

53. They are enemies of Christ and of the pope, who bid the Word of God be altogether silent in some Churches, in order that pardons may be preached in others.

54. Injury is done the Word of God when, in the same sermon, an equal or a longer time is spent on pardons than on this Word.

55. It must be the intention of the pope that if pardons, which are a very small thing, are celebrated with one bell, with single processions and ceremonies, then the Gospel, which is the very greatest thing, should be preached with a hundred bells, a hundred processions, a hundred ceremonies.

56. The "treasures of the Church," out of which the pope grants indulgences, are not sufficiently named or known among the people of Christ.

57. That they are not temporal treasures is certainly evident, for many of the vendors do not pour out such treasures so easily, but only gather them.

58. Nor are they the merits of Christ and the Saints, for even without the pope, these always work grace for the inner man, and the cross, death, and hell for the outward man.

59. St. Lawrence said that the treasures of the Church were the Church's poor, but he spoke according to the usage of the word in his own time.

60. Without rashness we say that the keys of the Church, given by Christ's merit, are that treasure;

61. For it is clear that for the remission of penalties and of reserved cases, the power of the pope is of itself sufficient.

62. The true treasure of the Church is the Most Holy Gospel of the glory and the grace of God.

63. But this treasure is naturally most odious, for it makes the first to be last.

64. On the other hand, the treasure of indulgences is naturally most acceptable, for it makes the last to be first.

65. Therefore the treasures of the Gospel are nets with which they formerly were wont to fish for men of riches.

66. The treasures of the indulgences are nets with which they now fish for the riches of men.

67. The indulgences which the preachers cry as the "greatest graces" are known to be truly such, in so far as they promote gain.

68. Yet they are in truth the very smallest graces compared with the grace of God and the piety of the Cross.

69. Bishops and curates are bound to admit the commissaries of apostolic pardons, with all reverence.

70. But still more are they bound to strain all their eyes and attend with all their ears, lest these men preach their own dreams instead of the commission of the pope.

71. He who speaks against the truth of apostolic pardons, let him be anathema and accursed!

72. But he who guards against the lust and license of the pardon-preachers, let him be blessed!

73. The pope justly thunders against those who, by any art, contrive the injury of the traffic in pardons.

74. But much more does he intend to thunder against those who use the pretext of pardons to contrive the injury of holy love and truth.

75. To think the papal pardons so great that they could absolve a man even if he had committed an impossible sin and violated the Mother of God—this is madness.

76. We say, on the contrary, that the papal pardons are not able to remove the very least of venial sins, so far as its guilt is concerned.

77. It is said that even St. Peter, if he were now Pope, could not bestow greater graces; this is blasphemy against St. Peter and against the pope.

78. We say, on the contrary, that even the present pope, and any pope at all, has greater graces at his disposal; to wit, the Gospel, powers, gifts of healing, etc., as it is written in 1 Corinthians 12.

79. To say that the cross, emblazoned with the papal arms, which is set up [by the preachers of indulgences], is of equal worth with the Cross of Christ, is blasphemy.

80. The bishops, curates, and theologians who allow such talk to be spread among the people, will have an account to render.

81. This unbridled preaching of pardons makes it no easy

matter, even for learned men, to rescue the reverence due to the pope from slander, or even from the shrewd questionings of the laity.

82. To wit:—"Why does not the pope empty purgatory, for the sake of holy love and of the dire need of the souls that are there, if he redeems an infinite number of souls for the sake of miserable money with which to build a Church? The former reasons would be most just; the latter is most trivial."

83. Again:—"Why are mortuary and anniversary masses for the dead continued, and why does he not return or permit the withdrawal of the endowments founded on their behalf, since it is wrong to pray for the redeemed?"

84. Again:—"What is this new piety of God and the pope, that for money they allow a man who is impious and their enemy to buy out of purgatory the pious soul of a friend of God, and do not rather, because of that pious and beloved soul's own need, free it for pure love's sake?"

85. Again:—"Why are the penitential canons long since in actual fact and through disuse abrogated and dead, now satisfied by the granting of indulgences, as though they were still alive and in force?"

86. Again:—"Why does not the pope, whose wealth is to-day greater than the riches of the richest, build just this one church of St. Peter with his own money, rather than with the money of poor believers?"

87. Again:—"What is it that the pope remits, and what participation does he grant to those who, by perfect contrition, have a right to full remission and participation?"

88. Again:—"What greater blessing could come to the Church than if the pope were to do a hundred times a day what he now does once, and bestow on every believer these remissions and participations?"

89. "Since the pope, by his pardons, seeks the salvation of souls rather than money, why does he suspend the indulgences and pardons granted heretofore, since these have equal efficacy?"

90. To repress these arguments and scruples of the laity by force alone, and not to resolve them by giving reasons, is to expose the Church and the pope to the ridicule of their enemies, and to make Christians unhappy.

91. If, therefore, pardons were preached according to the spirit and mind of the pope, all these doubts would be readily resolved; nay, they would not exist.

92. Away, then, with all those prophets who say to the people of Christ, "Peace, peace," and there is no peace!

93. Blessed be all those prophets who say to the people of Christ, "Cross, cross," and there is no cross!

94. Christians are to be exhorted that they be diligent in following Christ, their Head, through penalties, deaths, and hell;

95. And thus be confident of entering into heaven rather through many tribulations, than through the assurance of peace.

Compiled and annotated by
Reverend Jonathon Bakker and
Reverend Kenneth Bomberger

Any foray into Martin Luther's life invariably whets an appetite to learn more. Whether it is information about his life, teachings, opponents, or the political climate around him—it all makes for intriguing study. The following works are but a starting point for those interested in reading more about Martin Luther. They include annotated bibliographies and will help the reader further along in their search for Luther.

Luther's Life

•

Bainton, Roland H. *Here I Stand: A Life of Martin Luther.* New York: Abingdon-Cokesbury, 1950. 422 pages.

This volume, written in the mid-twentieth century, has remained over the years one of the most popular and informative biographies of Luther and an account of his enduring importance. Although a work of sound scholarship, *Here I Stand* is a readable work for the specialist and non-expert like.

Hendrix, Scott H. *Martin Luther: Visionary Reformer.* New Haven: Yale University Press, 2015. 341 pages.

This recent biography of Luther presents a picture of the reformer that draws on the latest scholarship devoted to Luther and his context. Its author presents a Luther who is both gifted and flawed in a well-balanced portrait. Luther's entire life in its personal, political, and theological dimensions is critically and fairly examined.

Markwald, Rudolf K., and Marilynn Morris Markwald. *Katharina Von Bora: A Reformation Life.* St. Louis: Concordia, 2002. 253 pages, paperback.

The first serious biography of Luther's wife, Katharina Von Bora. Well reviewed, this book offers a unique perspective on Martin Luther's home and family.

Nohl, Frederick. *Luther: Biography of a Reformer.* St. Louis: Concordia, 2003. 219 pages, hardcover.

Originally published in 1962 as *Martin Luther: Hero of Faith*, this volume was released in conjunction with the 2003 *Luther* film, which starred Joseph Fiennes as Martin Luther. Like many Luther biographies, plenty of attention is given to the early career of the Reformer, but Nohl does a fine job of highlighting significant elements of his mature life and work.

Paulson, Steven. *Luther for Armchair Theologians.* Louisville: Westminster John Knox Press, 2004. 224 pages, paperback.

A brief examination of Luther's life and a basic introduction to his understanding of the Christian faith and teaching, this book, punctuated with winsome illustrations, will appeal to a broad audience of young and old alike.

Saarnivaara, Uuras. *Luther Discovers the Gospel.* Eugene, OR: Wipf and Stock, 2003. 146 pages, paperback.

A limited and brief biography of Luther's life from his time as a monk until his "tower experience" in 1518. Saarnivaara includes a basic investigation into the significance of Augustine's theological influence on Luther.

Reformation History

Forde, Gerhard O. *On being a theologian of the Cross: Reflections on Luther's Heidelberg Disputation.* Grand Rapids: Wm. B. Eerdmans Publishing Co., 1997. 121 pages, paperback.

This book brings useful insight into what would become a pivotal matter in Luther's understanding of the human condition.

Kolb, Robert, and James A. Nestingen, eds. *Sources and Contexts of The Book of Concord.* Minneapolis: Fortress, 2001. 277 pages, paperback.

Kolb and Nestingen have contributed a valuable resource for Reformation scholars in providing English translations of several key documents related to the conflicts of Luther's life. Includes such works as Agricola's *One Hundred Thirty Common Questions* and the *Confutation of the Augsburg Confession.* A must for any serious inquiry into the multifaceted dynamics of Reformation history.

Lund, Eric, ed. *Documents from the History of Lutheranism, 1517-1750.* Minneapolis: Fortress, 2002. 330 pages, paperback.

Lund has gathered together a wealth of information related to the history of early Lutheranism, about half of which deals either directly or tangentially with Martin Luther. Writings by Luther, against Luther, and about Luther are found throughout this unique volume. These include sermons, hymns, satirical propaganda, and serious theological treatises. A must for those interested in digging deeper into Luther's background and opponents.

McGrath, Alister E. *Reformation Thought: An Introduction.* Third edition. Malden, MA: Blackwell, 2001. 329 pages, paperback.

McGrath's useful survey is helpful for readers interested in the broader climate of the Reformation. Luther and his theology are only one facet of the Reformation and this book fills in much more of the details for readers seeking to understand the complexities and figures involved in the Reformation era, including Radical Reformers and Roman Catholic opponents.

Pettegree, Andrew. *Brand Luther: How an Unheralded Monk Turned His Small Town into a Center of Publishing, Made Himself the Most Famous Man in Europe—and Started the Protestant Reformation.* New York: Penguin Press, 2015. 400 pages, hardcover.

Pettegree explores the role of the printing press in Luther's success, examining how Luther's recognition of the hidden potential of printing helped his message spread like wildfire and turned him into a mass-media figure.

Schwiebert, Ernest G. *The Reformation.* Minneapolis: Fortress Press, 1996. 598 pages, hardcover.

This volume by a historian of the sixteenth century is an examination of the Reformation in its German and university settings. Special attention is given to how Luther and the Reformation transformed the university and its educational mission in Germany.

Spitz, Lewis W. *The Renaissance and Reformation Movements.* Volume II: *The Reformation.* Revised edition. St. Louis: Concordia, 1987. 614 pages, paperback.

Spitz's classic study of the Reformation puts it in context with the preceding Renaissance, and thoroughly considers religious impact across Europe. It includes a discussion of the societal and cultural effects. It is careful with details, and is well researched and written.

Wellman, Sam. *Frederick the Wise: Seen and Unseen Lives of Martin Luther's Protector.* St. Louis: Concordia, 2015. 352 pages, paperback.

This volume presents the life of a key figure and powerful early defender of Martin Luther and his teachings. Among other achievements, Frederick founded the University of Wittenberg in 1501, where Luther famously taught.

Luther's Theology

Bayer, Oswald. *Martin Luther's Theology: A Contemporary Interpretation.* Trans. Thomas H. Trapp. Grand Rapids: Eerdmans, 2008. 374 pages, paperback.

A modern academic appraisal of Luther's theology from one of the foremost Luther scholars of the 20th century. Bayer's appraisal is thoroughly systematic and pastoral. Though not as easily read by laypeople as other volumes, it is an excellent representation of current Luther scholarship.

Braaten, Carl E. and Robert W. Jenson, eds. *Union with Christ: The New Finnish Interpretation of Luther.* Grand Rapids: Eerdmans, 1998, 182 pages, paperback.

This collection of essays makes available to English readers the results of Finnish interpretations of Luther's theology. Four Finnish theologians associated with this reinterpretation of Luther are represented here as well as four American theologians who critique the new understanding of Luther's Christology.

Klug, Eugene F. A. *Lift High This Cross: The Theology of Martin Luther.* St. Louis: Concordia, 2003. 176 pages, paperback.

A blend of biography and theology, Klug's volume communicates Luther's theology by investigating the key events in Luther's life and work. From the Ninety-Five Theses to the Diet at Worms to the writing and publication of the Smalcald Articles, the reader can easily grasp the central elements of Luther's theology. This work is very accessible for laypeople.

Kolb, Robert, and Charles P. Arand. *The Genius of Luther's Theology.* Grand Rapids: Baker, 2008. 240 pages, paperback.

This treatment of Luther's understanding of righteousness before God and man, and the implications this has for humanity, will appeal to the intellectual layman, and has insight for civil, social, and global events, as well as human life issues.

Kolb, Robert, Irene Dingel, and Lubomir Batka, eds. The *Oxford Handbook of Martin Luther's Theology.* New York: Oxford University Press, 2014. 688 pages, hardcover.

This collection of essays by historians and theologians explores Luther's thought in its historical context as well as its impact through the centuries. It also provides analyses of his hermeneutical principles and his theology. It is a helpful introductory guide to Luther scholarship.

Lienhard, Marc. *Luther: Witness to Jesus Christ.* Minneapolis: Ausburg Publishing House, 1982. 412 pages, hardcover.

This study, originally published in French, provides a detailed examination of a central part of Luther's theology and thought: his views of the person and work of Christ. The author shows how Luther develops his understanding of Christ in sermons, lectures, and commentaries over the curse of his life.

Lohse, Bernhard. *Martin Luther's Theology: Its Historical and Systematic Development.* Minneapolis: Fortress Press, 1999. 393 pages, hardcover.

Martin Luther was not a systematic theologian. Thus it is difficult to present an ordered treatment of Luther's thought, although many attempts have been made. The author of this volume traces the development of Luther's theological positions on a number of critical themes (e.g. sin, grace, Christ, law, and gospel).

Veith, Gene Edward, Jr. *The Spirituality of the Cross*. Revised edition. St. Louis: Concordia, 2010. 172 pages, paperback.

A contemporary volume on Lutheran spirituality written with a lay audience in mind. Veith helpfully organizes several key aspects of Luther's theology that many will find interesting, including the Means of Grace, his Doctrine of Vocation, and his Two Kingdom theology.

Wingren, Gustav. *Luther on Vocation*. Eugene, OR: Wipf and Stock, 2004. 268 pages, paperback.

For those interested in a much deeper and more substantive investigation into Luther's teachings on vocation, this book is highly recommended.

Luther's Writings

The Large Catechism, in Robert Kolb and Timothy J. Wengert, eds., *The Book of Concord: The Confessions of the Evangelical Lutheran Church*. Minneapolis: Fortress, 2000. 377-480, hardcover.

The Small Catechism, in Robert Kolb and Timothy J. Wengert, eds., *The Book of Concord: The Confessions of the Evangelical Lutheran Church*. Minneapolis: Fortress, 2000. 345-375, hardcover.

The Smalcald Articles, in Robert Kolb and Timothy J. Wengert, eds., *The Book of Concord: The Confessions of the Evangelical Lutheran Church*. Minneapolis: Fortress, 2000. 295-328, hardcover.

All three of the above writings constitute Luther's doctrinal contributions to the Evangelical Lutheran Church. They remain central to the theology and practice of Lutheran church bodies around the world to this day. This particular edition of the Book of Concord includes some helpful introductions from the editors.

Lull, Timothy F., and William R. Russell, eds. *Martin Luther's Basic Theological Writings.* 3rd ed. Minneapolis: Fortress Press, 2012. 755 pages, paperback.

There is no better way to learn Luther's theology and thinking than by reading his writings. Lull and Russell have skillfully curated a handy resource for introducing the uninitiated to some real highlights from Luther's hand. Writings are grouped together according to the general subject material, making this an excellent starting point for reading Luther.

Pelikan, Jaroslav, Helmut T. Lehmann, and Benjamin T. G. Mayes, eds. *Luther's Works.* American Edition. St. Louis: Concordia and Minneapolis: Fortress, various years, still in production. Multiple volumes.

For the serious student of Luther, the American Edition, which began as a joint project between Lutheran publishers, represents the most comprehensive English language collection of his writings.